Meaningful Outreach

AN ESSENTIAL GUIDE FOR CHURCHES

MARK A. WOOD

CONCORDIA PUBLISHING HOUSE · SAINT LOUIS

DEDICATION

To Mary Ellen, truly my helpmate.
Adam had Eve.
Martin had his Katie.
I've been blessed with you.

Published by Concordia Publishing House
3558 S. Jefferson Avenue, St. Louis, MO 63118-3968
1-800-325-3040 • cph.org

Manufactured in the United States of America

Library of Congress Cataloging-in-Publication Data

Names: Wood, Mark A., 1959- author.

Title: Making disciples through effective outreach / Mark A Wood.

Description: Saint Louis, MO : Concordia Publishing House, [2022] |

Identifiers: LCCN 2021062214 (print) | LCCN 2021062215 (ebook) | ISBN 9780758670595 (paperback) | ISBN 9780758670601 (ebook)

Subjects: LCSH: Discipling (Christianity) | Evangelistic work.

Classification: LCC BV4520 .W595 2022 (print) | LCC BV4520 (ebook) | DDC 269/.2--dc23/eng/20220216

LC record available at https://lccn.loc.gov/2021062214
LC ebook record available at https://lccn.loc.gov/2021062215

1 2 3 4 5 6 7 8 9 10   31 30 29 28 27 26 25 24 23 22

Table of Contents

INTRODUCTION

Has this ever happened to you?

You hold an outreach event at your congregation that brings people from the community to your campus, such as a dinner or Oktoberfest or a living nativity. Having thought it through, you provide attractive invitations to upcoming events at your church. You especially highlight a new Bible study series or special worship services.

You are thrilled when people from the community come and enjoy the event. They are grateful to the congregation for hosting it, and they have a good time. Members and guests mingle and have good conversations. The event is a success!

Later, at the new Bible study or special worship service, you eagerly wait for some of the people who came to the event to show up. But to your disappointment, not a single nonchurched person comes.

Why didn't they come? What did you do wrong?

The reason people didn't act on your invitation to a Bible study or worship service isn't in what you did wrong but in what you didn't do. Effective outreach doesn't happen through a single event but through an intentional process that guides people from a point of connection (such as an event) into the Word-and-Sacrament ministry of your congregation. It bridges the giant leap, as many nonchurched people see it, from enjoying a social event to participating in worship or Bible study.

How do I know this? I've experienced the disappointments of ineffective outreach. As a church planter in Florida, I approached outreach in an attractional, event-oriented manner. I hoped the nonchurched people at our Oktoberfest and living nativity events would come to our special worship services and Bible studies because we handed out colorful and engaging invitations. I was disappointed. Hundreds of people were invited, but not a single one accepted those invitations. I learned firsthand that splashy events, especially one-time events, don't make for effective outreach. I also learned what does make for effective outreach.

Through the ups and downs of my church-planting experiences, research on witness and outreach, and post-graduate studies, I came to understand that effective outreach is a process, not an event. That process may start with events, but it intentionally goes much further. It is centered in relationship building and focused on bringing the Means of Grace to people and people to the Means of Grace. I captured this process and summed it up as "Create Connections, Build Relationships, Make Disciples." In the intervening years, this outreach process has been further refined but remains fundamentally unchanged.

Learning and applying this outreach process isn't complicated or demanding. It takes some work, but mostly it takes a shift in perspective to see things from the nonchurched person's point of view. It's a process that everyone involved in the ministries and activities of your congregation—pastors, other church workers, lay leaders, board members, and so forth—can and should learn so that outreach isn't a task in addition to what you are already doing as a congregation but is an integral part of your congregation's mission and purpose.

It is my hope and prayer that you can make use of the outreach process and other ideas in this book to engage the nonchurched people in your community that they may be led into the Word-and-Sacrament ministry of your congregation. You won't find a magic wand to wave and make disciples. Instead, you will find practical ideas that you can adapt and apply in your context. Perhaps, under God's blessings, you will see your outreach efforts result in people becoming new disciples of Jesus Christ. It could happen in your congregation, just as it happened in mine when I used this outreach approach as a church planter and parish pastor.

—Pastor Mark A. Wood

WHAT IS OUTREACH?

> I have made you a light for the Gentiles, that you may bring salvation to the ends of the earth.   ACTS 13:47

"Everyone Welcome." The sign caught my eye. It was strategically placed in front of a building on a busy street. Thousands of people passed it every day. It clearly listed the meeting times so anyone could act on the invitation to join the people who had put up the sign. But I knew I would not attend the events, even though the sign assured me I was welcome.

Why? First, I wasn't interested in what they were offering. A long time ago, when I was young, I was very interested. But over time, I lost interest in those things and found other things that interested me more—things that I considered more

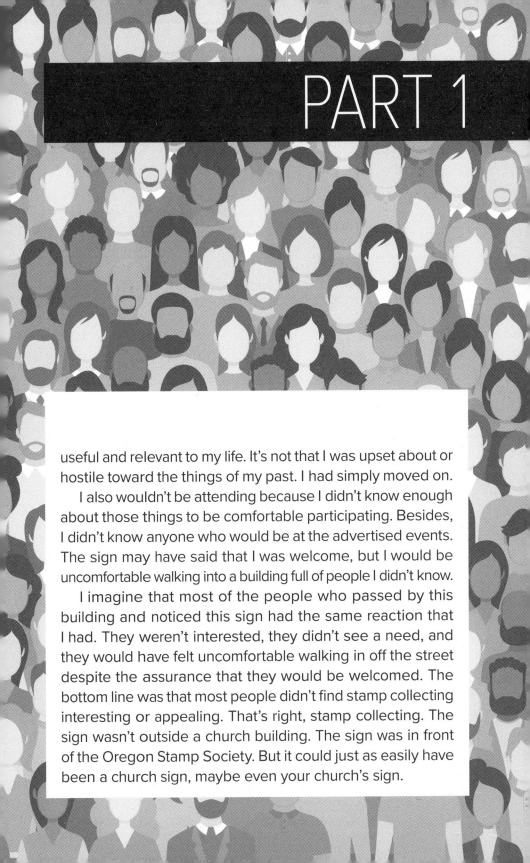

useful and relevant to my life. It's not that I was upset about or hostile toward the things of my past. I had simply moved on.

I also wouldn't be attending because I didn't know enough about those things to be comfortable participating. Besides, I didn't know anyone who would be at the advertised events. The sign may have said that I was welcome, but I would be uncomfortable walking into a building full of people I didn't know.

I imagine that most of the people who passed by this building and noticed this sign had the same reaction that I had. They weren't interested, they didn't see a need, and they would have felt uncomfortable walking in off the street despite the assurance that they would be welcomed. The bottom line was that most people didn't find stamp collecting interesting or appealing. That's right, stamp collecting. The sign wasn't outside a church building. The sign was in front of the Oregon Stamp Society. But it could just as easily have been a church sign, maybe even your church's sign.

CHAPTER 1

CALLING SOMETHING "OUTREACH"

For many congregations, a sign out front and a local advertisement with service times are the extent of their outreach efforts. They feel they've done their part by making people aware of what's available and assuring them that they are welcome. "They know where we are" is a statement I've heard some people say about their outreach efforts. They don't realize or may not care that the nonchurched people who pass by their signs or see their ads aren't interested, don't see a need, or would feel uncomfortable walking in off the street into a building full of strangers.

Many congregations put up a sign or post an advertisement and call it outreach. But calling something "outreach" doesn't make it outreach. That may seem obvious, but far too often a congregation's outreach efforts aren't really outreach at all. Some of those efforts may have started as outreach years ago, but they've morphed into events and activities that have little to do with outreach. Some never had anything to do with reaching lost people with the Gospel, but they were labeled as outreach and may have even been assigned to the Outreach Committee. Despite our best intentions and heartfelt desires, calling something "outreach" or assigning it to the Outreach Committee doesn't make it outreach.

What is it, then, that makes an event or activity outreach? More important, what makes something effective outreach? Answering these questions begins with understanding who we are and what we have been called to be and to do as priests in Christ's "royal priesthood" (1 Peter 2:9).

Our Call to Be Priests

> For priests, the baptized, and Christians are all one and the same. MARTIN LUTHER

Very few Christians in the Western Church today would call themselves priests. Instead, we have given that title to professional church workers. That's too bad. The word *priest* is one of the words that the Bible uses to help us understand who we are in Christ and what He has called us to do. Martin Luther wanted the word used to describe and define believers. He said, "It would please me very much if this word 'priest' were used as commonly as the term 'Christians' is applied to us. For priests, the baptized, and Christians are all one and the same."[1] Today we might add "disciple, believer, and Christ follower" to that list. We can substitute the word *priest* for whatever noun we use to describe a person who has faith in Jesus.

The word *priest* is a meaningful way to describe a Christian because it conveys an understanding of who we are in Christ that is deeply rooted in the Bible. In the Old Testament, the priests were a select group from among the people of Israel. In the New Testament, the limitations of the Old Testament priesthood have been lifted and God makes all His people priests. In both testaments, priests are not independent and isolated but are part of a greater whole called the priesthood. While Old Testament priests and New Testament priests serve in different ways, the purpose of the priesthood in both testaments is the same.

Every Christian is a priest in a new order of things ushered in by our Savior, Jesus. We are not priests in the order of Aaron, who had to offer blood sacrifices for the atonement of the sins of the priests and the people. We are priests of the New Covenant, in which we bring people the forgiveness won by the one, full, final sacrifice of Jesus on the cross.

---

1   *Luther's Works*, vol. 30, p. 63

The Purpose of the Priesthood

> But you are a chosen race, a royal priesthood, a holy nation, a people for His own possession, that you may proclaim the excellencies of Him who called you out of darkness into His marvelous light. 1 PETER 2:9

The purpose of the priesthood in the Old Testament was to offer the sacrifices that the Lord had prescribed. Most of the sacrifices were made as payment for sins against God. The priests would serve as mediators for the people who needed to make a sacrifice but, because of their sins, could not enter into the presence of a Holy God. The priests, because the Lord had made them priests, were able to approach God's altar and offer sacrifices on behalf of the people bringing them. After the sacrifices were made, the priest came back to the people with the good news that their sins were atoned for—they were forgiven through the blood of the sacrifice according to God's Word.

Our role as priests is also to stand between a Holy God and people who cannot approach Him. But we are not making blood sacrifices brought by people who trust in God's promises. Jesus, whom the Bible calls the "one mediator between God and men" (1 Timothy 2:5), made the full and final blood sacrifice for the sins of the whole world. As the people of Christ called by Him to be priests, we serve as His intermediaries for people who do not have faith in Him. We intercede for people before our Holy God in our prayers and, as we have the opportunity, we proclaim to them "the excellencies of Him who has called [us] out of darkness into His marvelous light" (1 Peter 2:9).

In our role as priests, we are intermediaries for the people who are lost in their sins and the gracious God who wants them to know His love and forgiveness. We carry out that work in two different but related ways. One way is through witnessing, which is our individual efforts to share God's Word with the lost people in our everyday lives. The other is through our collective efforts as a congregation to engage the nonchurched people in our community through our ministries and activities. This is called outreach.

CHAPTER 2

OUTREACH DEFINED

> And those servants went out into the roads and gathered all whom they found, both bad and good. So the wedding hall was filled with guests. MATTHEW 22:10

Jesus told a number of parables to explain the kingdom of heaven. One of those parables is recorded in Matthew 22:1–14. In this parable, Jesus likened the Kingdom to a wedding feast a king gave for his son. After the people who had been invited to the wedding feast refused to come, the king instructed his servants to go "to the main roads and invite to the wedding feast" (v. 9) as many people as they could find. So the servants "went out into the roads and gathered all whom they found, both bad and good" and the king's feast was filled with guests.

While Jesus told this parable to describe the Kingdom, it is also a very good illustration of our role in evangelism. Rather than seeing evangelism as a task that we undertake to "win souls" or convince people to become Christians, we should understand evangelism as the things we do to go into our world and invite people "both bad and good" to the marriage feast of the King's Son. Evangelism is what we do as God's servants for "the wedding hall [to be] filled with guests."

To properly understand evangelism and to effectively equip people for it, we need to make an important distinction between two aspects of evangelism. This distinction follows the two ways that we function as the Church. In some things, we function as the Church Gathered and in other things we function as the Church Scattered. The Church Gathered refers to the things we do when we are together. A common example of the Church Gathered is when we meet together for worship. But the Church Gathered is not limited to worship, and worship is not limited to the Church Gathered. When we come together to serve our community, raise funds for missions, conduct the business of our congregation, study God's Word, or a host of other things that bring us together, we are the Church Gathered.

The Church Scattered refers to the work we do when we are separated from one another. The term reminds us that we don't stop being the Church when we go our separate ways. Our work as the Church Scattered takes place in our homes, neighborhoods, schools, workplaces, ball fields, and many other places in our communities. Many congregations have a sign posted by an exit door or at the parking lot exit that says, "Now entering the mission field." This sign is meant to remind us to live out our callings as the Church Scattered while we go about our daily lives away from the other members of our congregation.

The distinction between the Church Gathered and the Church Scattered helps us see two aspects of evangelism. Evangelism that is related to the Church Scattered is called *witness*. Evangelism that is related to the Church Gathered is *outreach*. Because they are closely related, the words *witness* and *outreach* are often used interchangeably. But the distinction between *witness* and *outreach* is important. If we confuse the two, we may neglect one or both. Keeping them distinct but closely related will help us be more effective in both witness and outreach.

Witnessing is the work that we as God's priests carry out individually in our vocations. It takes place in our homes, neighborhoods, schools, workplaces, ball fields, and many other places in our communities—other than our church. Witnessing starts with the personal relationships that we have or develop with lost people.

Outreach is the work of the congregation to engage the non-churched people who live in the local community. Outreach starts where there is little or no relationship between the congregation and the lost people in the local community.

Outreach is most effective when it is integrated with witnessing. You'll do well to develop your skills in both witness and outreach.

In this book, we will focus on outreach. For witnessing, please make use of the resources available from Concordia Publishing House, including *Every One His Witness* and *Connected to Christ: Witnessing in Everyday Life*.

Let's start our discussion about effective outreach by looking at a working definition of the term.

Definition of Outreach

Outreach is not unique to churches. Businesses, community groups, and nonprofit organizations make use of outreach to carry out their missions. While the reasons for conducting outreach vary, the common thread in the secular world is to extend the product or service of the organization beyond its current limits. In other words, they use outreach to expand their market, audience, or constituency. The evangelistic outreach of a congregation also seeks to expand its reach beyond its current membership to share with more people what we have to offer—the love, joy, and peace of Jesus Christ.

To distinguish the evangelistic outreach of a congregation from the outreach that secular organizations conduct, we'll use the following definition of outreach:

> **Our congregation's efforts to make disciples by engaging the nonchurched people in our community through our ministries and activities in order to share the Gospel of Jesus Christ with them.**

There's a lot packed into this definition. Let's thoroughly examine it so we may better understand *outreach*.

OUTREACH: OUR CONGREGATION'S EFFORTS

Outreach is the work that we do as the Church Gathered. Outreach is planned and carried out by members of our congregation working in teams, as boards or committees, and as both small and large groups representing our congregation. Whether it takes place on our campus or somewhere else in our community, outreach is done in the name of our congregation.

This doesn't mean that there isn't a place for one-on-one interaction between members of our congregation and the nonchurched people we engage through outreach. If opportunities arise for our members to witness to lost people during our outreach efforts, we certainly want to encourage that. What it does mean is that the effort that brings about the opportunity for witnessing has been planned and conducted by our congregation.

OUTREACH: MAKE DISCIPLES

When I ask church leaders why they want to be more effective in their outreach efforts, they often explain that they need more members, want more people to help out, or hope to increase giving to "make the budget." While these are not bad things, they aren't good motives for conducting outreach. In the first place, they are self-centered. They are about what we want and what benefits us. Second, they are confusing the work of the Holy Spirit with the work we are called to do.

The proper motive for outreach is found in the Great Commission. Jesus calls us, His Church, to make disciples. Our joy-filled response to all that Christ has done for us is to gladly do what we can to bring the Gospel to people who don't know the love, joy, and peace of Jesus. Our role in making disciples is to plant and water. Planting and watering should be the focus of our outreach efforts, and making disciples should be the outcome that we desire.

Unfortunately, other things can become the driving force behind our outreach efforts. Congregations that are experiencing decline may be motivated to conduct outreach activities to increase membership, get more people in the pews, overcome budget shortfalls, or find more people to pitch in to get the work of the congregation done. We should understand that these things are potential fruits of conducting outreach, not the reasons for doing it.

OUTREACH: NONCHURCHED PEOPLE

Outreach is focused on engaging nonchurched people—people who do not have a connection to a Christian church. Outreach is not about building fellowship with members of other Lutheran congregations or convincing members of non-Lutheran Christian churches to become Lutherans. If someone is an active member of another Christian congregation, he is churched. We are not trying to engage churched people through our outreach efforts. We have other activities to do that. Outreach is about reaching nonchurched people.

I was discussing outreach opportunities for a declining congregation with one of the lay leaders. He explained that the large Baptist and Methodist churches were attracting all the Christians in their area. Knowing the demographics of the community, I pointed out that over half of the people who lived near the church did not belong to any Christian congregation. The Baptists and Methodists were not their competition. There were plenty of nonchurched people to reach with the Gospel. Their actual "competition" was Satan, who held those people captive to sin and death.

The term *nonchurched* is a helpful descriptor of the people we want to reach, but we should never forget what it means for someone to be nonchurched. Whether a person is nonchurched because she is dechurched (once connected to a Christian church but no longer) or is unchurched (never connected to a Christian church), a nonchurched person is lost. She is cut off from Christ. She is perishing. She needs us to reach out to her with the treasures that Jesus has entrusted to us. Nonchurched people are the object of our outreach.

OUTREACH: IN OUR COMMUNITY

One of the most damaging things that we can do to the outreach efforts of our congregation is to confuse distant missions with outreach. Outreach is always local. Our outreach takes place in the community in which our congregation exists. If we go on a mission trip and are involved in outreach efforts as part of that experience, our work is not our outreach but is supporting someone else's outreach. It's their outreach in their community. Our outreach takes place in our community.

It's important to know what we mean by "our community." Keeping in mind that outreach is the work we do as the Church Gathered, outreach happens in and around our congregation's physical location. Because all our members may not live, work, and play in this physical location, they may conduct witness as the Church Scattered in other places.

Congregations end up located where they are for many different reasons, but all are where they are for the same purpose: to bring God's Word to the mission field where He has placed them. However our congregation has come to be where it is, the community around our congregation's campus is the mission field that the Lord has called us to reach out to. There may be more attractive mission fields, easier mission fields, or more exciting mission fields, but God has placed our congregation in this place, at this time, for these people. We are, with the people around us, a community.

OUTREACH: ENGAGING THROUGH OUR MINISTRIES AND ACTIVITIES

Engaging refers to active and intentional interaction between human beings. When we talk and serve, we are engaging with others. The word *engaging* underscores the active—not passive—nature of outreach. We aren't being faithful in outreach if all we do is put up a sign or run an ad and wait for people to show up. While advertising and marketing are part of our outreach efforts (something we'll discuss later), in and of themselves they are ineffective ways of reaching people in our community. We know this because we are often the targets of advertising and marketing. Every day companies, organizations, and other groups are vie for our attention through various forms of advertising and marketing. Despite their best efforts, we ignore most of it. Think about the advertisements that you receive. What do you do with the glossy fliers in your mailbox? How much attention do you pay to the advertisements that interrupt the music on the radio or streaming service? How often do you click on a pop-up ad on your computer?

Most advertising is ignored because it is passive. Advertising and marketing that engages people tends to be more effective than advertising that expects the recipient to take action. In much the same way, effective outreach involves engaging people through our congregation's ministries and activities rather than simply sharing information and expecting people to take action. In other words, outreach is not passive; we actively and intentionally conduct outreach through our ministries and activities.

What does the phrase "ministries and activities" mean? The word *ministry* has both narrow and wide senses. Some people are comfortable using the word broadly and see many different things in the congregation as ministries. Other people prefer to use the word in a narrow sense and to refer only to things directly related to Word-and-Sacrament ministry as ministry. In the New Testament, the word *diakonia* can be translated as "ministry" (its verbal form is *diakoneo*). We find the word used in both a wide sense and a narrow sense in various passages. In Acts 1:25, Peter used the word in its narrow sense as he led the apostles in choosing Matthias to replace Judas in "this ministry (*diakonia*) and apostleship." In Acts 6:4, we find the word used in its narrow sense right after the verb is used in its wide sense in verse 2. The wide sense is also used in Luke 10:40, when Martha complained to Jesus, "Lord, do you not care that my sister has left me to serve (*diakoneo*) alone?" The phrase "ministries and activities" is meant to capture both senses of the word *ministry*. It refers to all the things that our congregation does to serve people inside and outside of the Church.

Outreach: To Share the Gospel of Jesus Christ

In Romans 10:17, we are told plainly that people come to faith through the Word of God. "Faith comes from hearing, and hearing through the word of Christ." This means that the only way someone can become a disciple of Jesus is through God's Word. It's a serious mistake to think that showing someone the love of Jesus through acts of mercy or other forms of service is enough for them to become disciples. We must always aim to speak the love of Jesus through our outreach efforts.

This doesn't mean that we shouldn't do acts of mercy, provide human care, or serve our neighbors in other ways. On the contrary, these activities are good ways to show care and compassion to the people in our community. They often create opportunities for us to speak the love of Jesus to people outside our church. Effective outreach makes use of ministries and activities that are not Word-and-Sacrament ministry to invite nonchurched people into our Word-and-Sacrament ministry.

We read in 1 Peter 3:15 to "always [be] prepared to make a defense to anyone who asks you for a reason for the hope that is in you." Through the various ways that we serve our neighbors in the love and joy of Jesus, we are opening doors for people to ask us about the hope that is within us. That may come as a question: "Why are you doing this?" or "What do you get out of this?" Whatever the question might be, it gives us an opportunity to share the Word of Christ. Effective outreach not only works to create these opportunities but it also ensures that we are prepared to faithfully respond to them.

I was visiting a congregation that had done a lot of great things to position themselves for outreach. After years of planning, preparations, and sacrifices, they had built a community center with facilities for several sports. People from the community were coming to the facility to participate in a variety of activities, from soccer to volleyball to the martial arts. That Sunday morning, the pastor told a story about a dechurched man who had come to the facility earlier that week for a sporting event. When he realized that it was a church facility, the man told the pastor he was impressed that a church would do something like this for the community. The pastor beamed with pride as he related the experience. Then he told the congregation, "The building hugged him." That is where the story ended.

Despite their willingness to reach out to their community and all the work that they had done to create a venue for attracting nonchurched people, they didn't have a plan to intentionally engage the people who came to use their facilities. As a result, they didn't have a way to obtain contact information for follow-up, and they were not prepared to invite people to ongoing activities to further relationships. They had hoped that people who came for the sporting activities would be curious enough about the church to come back on Sundays on their own to see what the church was all about. Their outreach approach was passive and ineffective.

How sad for this dechurched man. His opinion of churches had improved, but nothing had changed in his spiritual life. He didn't hear the Word of Christ. No one seized the opportunity to speak the love of Jesus to him. Even if "the building hugged him," hugs don't make disciples. Faith makes a person a disciple of Jesus, and faith comes from hearing the Word of Christ.

CHAPTER 3

WHAT MAKES FOR EFFECTIVE OUTREACH?

> What then is Apollos? What is Paul? Servants through whom you believed, as the Lord assigned to each. I planted, Apollos watered, but God gave the growth. 1 CORINTHIANS 3:5–6

Talking about outreach being effective can take us onto thin ice if we're not careful. We shouldn't use numbers to measure how effective our outreach efforts are because we are not in control of the results. As 1 Corinthians 3 reminds us, we can plant and we can water but we cannot make things grow. Measuring the effectiveness of our outreach efforts by how many people get baptized, are confirmed, attend worship services, and so forth is dangerously confusing our work with the work of the Holy Spirit. Instead, effective outreach focuses us on doing what we can to plant and water faithfully, not on producing the desired results. Keeping our focus on planting and watering guards us against resorting to human efforts to make disciples.

What does faithful planting and watering through effective outreach involve? It is like and unlike the farmer in the parable Jesus told in Matthew 13:1–9. In that parable, the farmer sowed seed without concerning himself with what kind of soil the seed was entering. He sowed generously and somewhat recklessly with the confidence that enough seed would fall into good soil for there to be a plentiful harvest. We share that confidence when we engage nonchurched people in our community. Like the parable's sower, we want to be generous in our sowing. But the field in which we are sowing is very different than the field of the parable. Contextually, we can surmise that the field in the parable would have been prepared for sowing. The farmer would have plowed and tilled the soil before sowing it. For the most part, we are in communities that are fallow fields of hard soil that need to be plowed and tended before we can sow generously.

Effective outreach starts with understanding and addressing the field of our community as it truly is. It involves preparing the soil and then sowing with intention. It also includes assessing what kind of planting and watering we are capable of doing as a congregation. I was raised in northern Illinois, but I've spent most of my adult life living in Florida and Arizona. While I'm not much of a gardener, I realize that what you can grow and how you grow it is different in each of these regions. The plants that grow well in the rich soil of the Midwest during the long summer days shrivel up and die in the desert heat of Arizona. Plants are already harvested in Florida before they are planted in Illinois. The citrus trees that prosper in the Sun Belt are nonexistent in northern regions. Everything is contextual. That's also true of effective outreach. What works well in one community may not work at all in another.

Because outreach is contextual, there is not a single way to do outreach effectively. However, there are some characteristics of effective outreach that apply in every context. Applying and adapting these characteristics will help your congregation better understand how to plan and conduct outreach more effectively in the field where the Lord has placed you and called you to plant and water.

Characteristics of Effective Outreach

Effective outreach seeks a healthy balance between "gathering" and "shepherding."

Outreach isn't the only activity to which Jesus has called us in His Great Commission. The two-fold call to make disciples directs us to serve two different groups of people. The first group are those outside the Church. We are to evangelize the lost people in our community. Another way to describe this work is to "gather the scattered." This work requires us to have an outward focus—to consider how we can share God's Word with people who are dechurched or unchurched. The second group are those who have been gathered into the Church and are active in worship, Bible study, and service. We are to care for the sheep that make up the flock that is our congregation. This aspect of our work under the Great Commission is called "shepherding the gathered."

There are other ways to refer to this two-fold work. Some people distinguish between these efforts by calling them "mission" and "maintenance." Others prefer calling the terms "outward-focused ministry" and "inward-focused ministry." Whatever we call the two ways in which we carry out our work, we cannot neglect one or the other. In other words, we can't pick or choose which of these works we are going to do. We are called to do both.

Faithfully working to "gather the lost" and "shepherd the gathered" is going to create tension in the congregation. Much of the tension will result because the congregation has limited resources to do its work. Some people might want to focus those resources on taking care of the congregation's members. Others may want to make witness, outreach, and mercy work higher priorities. The tension is unavoidable, but it is manageable when the leaders and members of the congregation work together to find, establish, and maintain the proper balance between "mission" and "maintenance" for their congregation in its context. In most cases, a healthy balance between an "outward focus" and an "inward focus" is going to be an overall focus that is slightly more outward than inward. Such a balance reflects our commitment to reach out to the nonchurched people in our community without neglecting the needs of our members.

Reaching agreement on what it will take and what it looks like to balance "gathering the lost" and "shepherding the gathered" is best achieved through developing a realistic and executable Strategic Ministry Plan through a consensus-based strategic planning process.[2]

---

2   An example of a consensus-based strategic planning process is found in the *re:Vitality* resource "Serving in God's Mission," available from the LCMS Office of National Mission.

EFFECTIVE OUTREACH CONSIDERS THE SHAPE OF THE COMMUNITY IN WHICH THE CONGREGATION EXISTS

Every community is unique. That means that your community is unique. It is made up of a mixture of people, businesses, organizations, traditions, and history that cannot be duplicated anywhere else. One of the least effective and most frustrating approaches to outreach is to take something that worked in someone else's community and attempt to use it "out of the box" in your community. Occasionally this "cookie cutter" approach works, but most of the time even the best programs have to be tailored for a congregation's specific context in order for them to be effective. A unique community calls for a unique plan for conducting outreach.

The starting point of creating a unique plan for outreach in your community is to make sure that you understand your community as it actually exists. Communities are not static. People move in and out of homes. Businesses open and close. The culture of a community changes over time through the influences of changing neighborhoods, aging of the residents, gentrification, technology, and other factors. Unless you've taken an objective look recently, your community may have changed in ways that you are not aware of.

I was once being interviewed by a call committee for a declining congregation seeking a new pastor. In preparation for the interview, I had assessed the shape of the community in which the congregation had existed for over fifty years. I noticed that the Hispanic population had significantly increased over the previous decade. When I asked the committee members what the congregation was doing to reach out to the nonchurched Hispanic people in their community, they replied that there weren't many Hispanic people in their neighborhood. The shape of their community had changed, but they did not recognize that it had.

Outreach is not going to be effective if it is planned and carried out with an outdated understanding of the shape of the community. Thankfully, it isn't difficult to assess the current shape of your community. One of the most helpful tools is a demographic report. Using United States Census Bureau data, marketing information, and data from other sources, demographic reports paint an accurate picture of the social, ethnic, racial, and economic makeup of a community. These reports are easily accessible and affordable[3].

As helpful as demographic reports are, they tell only part of a community's story. For a fuller picture of the shape of your community, you can contact organizations that are willing to share insights about the community. For example, your local chamber of commerce can provide useful information about the economic realities of the area and how they are impacting your community. Keep in mind that your congregation isn't the only organization that is interested in the shape of your community. It is likely that your city or county government has done studies and that you can request copies of those studies. While local social service agencies may not have done any formal studies, they have a wealth of information about your community through the interactions that they have with the people whom they serve.

Don't overlook a simple and effective way of learning about the people who live around your church: talk with them. There are several ways that you can start these conversations. Some are incidental conversations that happen while you are doing other things, such as conducting a prayer walk or working at a community event. Others are more intentional, such as going door-to-door in a canvass of your neighborhood. Many unexpected and fruitful conversations have started with a simple greeting and making time to talk with your neighbors.

EFFECTIVE OUTREACH EXPLORES NEW WAYS OF CREATING CONNECTIONS WITH NONCHURCHED PEOPLE

Expanding your congregation's reach into your community is usually more about being creative than it is about having a special program or unique skills. This is especially true if you're doing the same things for outreach repeatedly. An outreach activity that

---

3   Free demographic reports are available to anyone through the United States Census Bureau. Visit the Bureau's website at www.census.gov to access the latest census data. Many congregations of The Lutheran Church—Missouri Synod can request more detailed and focused demographic reports through their district offices at little or no cost to the congregation. For more information, contact your district office and request assistance with Mission InSite® reports.

may have been effective twenty years ago is probably not very effective anymore. Some of the things we do under the banner of outreach may draw a crowd of churched people, but they are of little interest to the nonchurched people around us.

If your congregation is in an outreach rut, it's time to think about new ways to connect with the nonchurched people in your community. One way to reach new people is by meeting an unmet need in your community. Rather than plan a new activity or event based on what churched people would like, plan the activity or event based on the needs and interests of the nonchurched people around you. If you don't know what unmet needs might be in your community, go back to the previous point about effective outreach and do some work to better understand the shape of your community.

Getting involved in your community is also a good way to discover new ideas to create connections with the nonchurched people. That involvement might come through a partnership between your congregation and a community group or civic organization. It could also be through offering your facilities to groups that need a place to meet or for a community event. Consider the ways in which members are already involved in the community and the organizations to which they already belong to see how their existing relationships might open doors for your congregation.

Above all, be creative and be willing to try things that may not be successful. Don't let the self-imposed limitations of "We tried that before and it didn't work" and "We've never done something like that before" keep you from trying new ways of creating connections with the nonchurched people in your community.

EFFECTIVE OUTREACH RECOGNIZES THAT CHURCHES DON'T BUILD RELATIONSHIPS, PEOPLE DO

Effective outreach is conducted through different kinds of relationships. The first kind of relationship is between our congregation and our community. We could call this a corporate relationship. It takes place at the organizational level. Corporate relationships are made and maintained between our congregation and individual people as well as between our congregation and other organizations in our community. This kind of relationship is helpful for creating connections with the nonchurched people around us, but it isn't the most important kind of relationship for effective outreach.

The second kind of relationship necessary for effective outreach is very different. Instead of being built through our congregational efforts, these relationships are created and nurtured at a personal level. They come from personal interaction between members of our congregation and the nonchurched people we connect with through our corporate relationships. Even though these relationships are formed at a personal level, they are not personal relationships like a friendship or a family relationship. They may become friendships as they mature, and we hope that they become members of our church family. For clarity, we'll refer to these relationships as outreach relationships.

Building outreach relationships tends to be the most challenging part of outreach for many congregations. One reason is that congregations often try to build outreach relationships, which are person-to-person in nature, in the same way that they try to build corporate relationships. In other words, they approach building personal relationships as an organization. That doesn't work well because organizations (including congregations) don't build personal relationships. It takes a person to build a personal relationship. The bottom line is that churches don't build relationships, people do.

It can be tempting to try to build relationships with nonchurched people through an organizational approach because it requires less commitment, less training, and fewer people. It is easier to manage. But it doesn't work well at all because churches don't build relationships, people do. Relationship building requires the commitment and involvement of members who are willing to invest themselves in the people we are able to make connections with.

Developing and nurturing relationships with the nonchurched people in our community is a critical part of effective outreach. It's also the part of outreach that is most often neglected by congregations. Why? First, we don't equip our members to develop and nurture relationships with the nonchurched people. Second, we fail to see the need to take the time and make the effort to build relationships. While relationship building is slow and hard work, it is often the most enriching and rewarding part of outreach. But because it is slow and difficult to do well, we're tempted to try to build relationships organizationally, even though churches don't build relationships, people do.

EFFECTIVE OUTREACH PROVIDES ONGOING ACTIVITIES THAT ENGAGE NONCHURCHED PEOPLE WITH OUR MEMBERS

While it is true that churches don't build relationships, people do, our congregation does have a very important role in building relationships by providing venues for ongoing interaction between our members and the nonchurched people in our community. Having events and activities that create the opportunity for ongoing interaction between church members and the people we connect with is vital to developing and nurturing relationships. The key to doing this effectively is in the words *ongoing* and *interaction*.

In the first place, the activity needs to create or facilitate inter-action between the nonchurched people and our members. We might have a great activity that many nonchurched people find interesting and appealing, but it won't help build relationships if none of our members attend or participate. It also won't be effec-tive if our members group together and stay to themselves during the activity or if they are so busy working on the activity that they can't interact with the nonchurched people who are present.

I was visiting a congregation in the Midwest to conduct an outreach workshop. During the workshop, we were discuss-ing what the congregation was already doing for outreach. For the most part, their outreach efforts were concentrated on one event. At this event, the congregation served a free Thanksgiving dinner for the community. It was a successful event in terms of attracting people. In their town of 20,000 or so residents, more than 1,000 people attended the dinner. When I asked about what they were doing during the event to foster relationship building, they explained they were so busy serving dinners that they didn't have time to interact with the people who attended. While the event was worthwhile because the congregation expressed care and concern for its community by serving the dinner, it wasn't an effective means of outreach because it didn't provide a way for members and nonchurched people to interact.

Even if the congregation had figured out a way to interact with the nonchurched people who came to their Thanksgiving dinner, it still would have fallen short of being effective for outreach because it lacked the second key element for building relationships. It was an annual event rather than an ongoing activity. Relationships blossom over time and through repeated interactions. Periodic events like Oktoberfests, spring flings, Thanksgiving dinners, and living nativities are great for creating connections with nonchurched people but they fall short of being effective relationship-building activities. We call these events and activities "one and done."

The problem with "one and done" activities and events is that they don't provide the time and interaction it takes to develop a relationship. Imagine a young couple going on their first date. Everything is going well. They really enjoy each other's company, and they discover many common interests. Toward the end of their time together, the young man tells the young lady that he is very much enjoying their date. He explains that this is the best first date he has ever had. She replies that she is also enjoying their date and is pleased with how well it has gone. Then, to her shock and amazement, the young man says to her, "That's great. Based on this date, I think we should get married. Would you marry me?" How do you think that young lady is going to respond to his spontaneous proposal? How might she respond if he asks her for a second date instead? How would her reaction be different if he proposed to her after several dozen dates instead of on their first date?

As silly as this first-date story is, it reflects how many congregations approach outreach. At or after a single relationship-building event or activity, the congregation invites the nonchurched person to come to worship or join a Bible study. From a nonchurched person's perspective, it's like being proposed to on a first date. Relationships take time and require ongoing interaction between people—and not just any people but the same nonchurched people interacting with the same church members over time.

EFFECTIVE OUTREACH EQUIPS AND ENCOURAGES MEMBERS TO SEEK NEW RELATIONSHIPS

There are several things that keep our members from building relationships with nonchurched people. One of the most common is that they are not properly equipped to build new relationships. Some people are naturally gifted in this, but most people are not. It's not that they don't want to build relationships with nonchurched people or that they don't realize how important it is, it's that they feel inadequate or uncomfortable when they try. They need training and support to learn how to start and develop relationships with the nonchurched people we make connections with. Unfortunately, few church leaders recognize the need for this kind of training and support—and even fewer do something to address it. Instead, they make the mistake of leaving relationship-building to the few people in the congregation for whom it comes naturally or who have been trained for it elsewhere.

Relying on a few people to build relationships not only discourages members from starting and developing relationships with nonchurched people but it also creates tenuous bonds between nonchurched people and our congregation. Instead of new people strengthening their connection with the congregation, they end up building a strong bond with the person with whom they have the relationship. If something happens to end that relationship, the nonchurched person's connection to the congregation is often lost. Because many congregations leave relationship building to the pastor, this often happens when the congregation's pastor retires, takes a new call, or passes away.

The first congregation I served as a pastor experienced the tragic loss of the pastor who had served them for more than twenty years. He was outgoing, gregarious, and a natural relationship builder. By default, he was the primary person in the congregation who started and developed relationships with people who were new to the congregation. Over the years, he had created and sustained hundreds of relationships, many of them with people who were previously nonchurched. When he died, most of those relationships died with him. Almost instantly, worship attendance and Bible study attendance dropped, and the number of inactive members increased. The people who remained had forged relationships and friendships with other members of the congregation apart from their relationships with the pastor. They had strong bonds to the congregation and were committed to continue the ministry of the congregation under the leadership of a new pastor.

Effective outreach depends on broadening the relationships that start with one person or a few people into relationships with many people in the congregation. This means that we need to equip many people in our congregation to begin and to nurture relationships with the nonchurched people we connect with. Not only do we need to train our members in relationship building but we also need to develop and foster an environment that supports and encourages relationship building. In other words, we should aim to make relationship building with new people a part of who we are as a congregation.

Here are some things we can do to make relationship building an integral part of our congregation's culture:

- Teach the importance of relationships as an element of making disciples.

- Promote relationship building as an important activity in one's own discipleship.

- Incorporate practical relationship-building actions into our existing activities (e.g., encouraging members to sit with non-churched visitors at our dinners).

- Recognize members who are demonstrating the kind of relationship building that contributes to effective outreach.

- Integrate relationship building into all aspects of the congregation's life.

Moving relationship building from an activity of a few people for whom it comes naturally to an integral part of how we carry out our work as a congregation is facilitated by an outreach approach that equips and encourages members to seek new relationships.

EFFECTIVE OUTREACH RELIES ON THE HOLY SPIRIT
TO MAKE DISCIPLES THROUGH THE MEANS OF GRACE

The desired outcome of our outreach efforts is that nonchurched people become disciples of Jesus Christ. However, that doesn't mean that we can measure the effectiveness of our outreach efforts by how many people become disciples. If we do, we've fallen into the grave error of thinking that we are the ones who can make disciples. As much as we may want people to become disciples of Jesus, the outcome of our outreach efforts is outside of our control. Only the Holy Spirit can make disciples.

Making disciples has become a popular topic among church leaders, Christian authors and speakers, and other influential people. As in anything that becomes popular in Christian circles, there are a wide variety of ideas about making disciples. Unfortunately, many of the most popular ideas put the focus of making disciples on us and what we do. There are even some who promote the idea that you're not a disciple yourself until you've made someone else a disciple! They focus disciple-making on human efforts as though we are able to do the "right things" to make people into disciples of Jesus. In contrast to these man-centered approaches to making disciples, Martin Luther emphasized our reliance on the Holy Spirit to make disciples in his explanation of the Third Article of the Apostles' Creed:

> I believe that I cannot by my own reason or strength believe in Jesus Christ, my Lord, or come to Him; but the Holy Spirit has called me by the Gospel, enlightened me with His gifts, sanctified and kept me in the true faith.
>
> In the same way He calls, gathers, enlightens, and sanctifies the whole Christian church on earth, and keeps it with Jesus Christ in the one true faith.

Just as we were not able to become disciples of Jesus by our efforts, we cannot make someone else a disciple of Jesus by what we do or what we get them to do. We are totally reliant on the Holy Spirit to work the faith that makes someone a disciple.

And that is good news for us! It means that we are not responsible for the results of outreach. We have been faithful when we have done what we can do through effective outreach even if it doesn't result in new disciples—though we certainly hope and pray that it does. We know that "the Holy Spirit . . . works faith, when and where it pleases God, in those who hear the good news."[4] While we don't know when or where the Holy Spirit will work to do this, we do know how. He "calls, gathers, enlightens, and sanctifies"[5] through the Means of Grace (i.e., Word and Sacrament) and He uses us as His instruments for bringing the Means of Grace to people and bringing people to the Means of Grace.

Effective outreach can't be measured in the number of new disciples as though we can control who and how many people become disciples of Jesus through the Means of Grace. But that doesn't mean that we can't measure the effectiveness of our outreach efforts. We can gauge the effectiveness of our outreach efforts by tracking how many nonchurched people we are able to make connections with, assessing their responses to our invitations to relationship-building activities, and evaluating which opportunities to enter into Word and Sacrament are of interest to nonchurched people. These gauges can also guide us in making adjustments so our outreach efforts are even more effective. Keep in mind that while we can do things to make our outreach efforts more effective, we cannot do or say anything to make the Means of Grace more effective. The Means of Grace are God's power unto salvation. They are never lacking anything necessary for making a nonbelieving person into a disciple of Jesus. Effective outreach embraces this truth and avoids anything that adds to or takes away from God's Word and Sacraments as being the only means for making disciples. The key to measuring the effectiveness of our outreach efforts is to remain centered on the Means of Grace and to trust the Holy Spirit to use the Means of Grace to make disciples when and where He wills.

---

4   Augsburg Confession, Article V, paragraph 2
5   Luther's Small Catechism, Apostles' Creed, Third Article

EFFECTIVE OUTREACH PROVIDES MULTIPLE POINTS OF ENTRY INTO WORD-AND-SACRAMENT MINISTRY

The Means of Grace are set. There is nothing other than God's Word and Sacraments that we can expect the Holy Spirit to use to create and sustain faith. This may seem limiting, but there are many different ways through which we can include people in the Word-and-Sacrament ministry of our congregation. Effective outreach involves developing creative and engaging ways to bring the Means of Grace to people and people to the Means of Grace. We can do this by providing nonchurched people with multiple entry points into our Word-and-Sacrament ministry.

When considering ways in which nonchurched people can enter into the Word-and-Sacrament ministry of our congregation, we need to take into account the perspective of the nonchurched people, the strength of the relationships that they have with members of our congregation, and which Word-and-Sacrament ministries are appropriate for them. It helps to put ourselves in the place of the nonchurched people we are inviting into the Means of Grace.

It's easy for us to project our perspective of our congregation onto other people. We know our congregation to be filled with people who are loving and caring. We find it to be a safe place filled with grace and centered in God's forgiveness. It is our place of refuge, comfort, and peace. But that isn't how many nonchurched people view churches. For some, a church is a foreign place far outside their frame of reference or experience. Others have had bad experiences in a church earlier in their lives. Many have a negative view of churches based on what they've learned through mass media or popular culture.

Given the unfavorable ways in which many nonchurched people view churches, we need to think through how they will perceive our invitations into the Word-and-Sacrament ministry of our congregation. We should recognize that people may be reluctant to come to a worship service or traditional Bible study because those activities are too unfamiliar and they feel uncomfortable coming to something they don't understand. So if the only ways that we offer the Means of Grace are through the Divine Service and Sunday morning Bible study, our outreach efforts are going to fall short of bringing people into the Word-and-Sacrament ministry through which the Holy Spirit makes disciples. That's not to say that all nonchurched people will respond unfavorably to an invitation to worship and Bible study. Some people, especially some dechurched people, may welcome an invitation to return to things that they miss and recognize as important to their lives.

What are some other entry points into the Word-and-Sacrament ministry of our congregation that we can offer to nonchurched people? They can either be things that we are already doing done in a new way or they can be new ministries or activities. Some examples of this include providing online access to worship services, making video or audio recordings of sermons and Bible studies available, holding an introductory Bible study in a nontraditional setting, editing Bible-study recordings to fit a podcast format, or conducting the adult instruction class or confirmation through online learning.

When I was having trouble getting people to commit to attending a twelve-week adult instruction class, I tried several things to improve participation. Nothing seemed to make much of a difference until I created an online, self-study version of the materials. By making the same content available in a new way, participation increased. People could take the class when it fit their schedules in the comfort of their own homes. We incorporated check points for gathering in person to discuss what we were learning and to provide the personal interaction that was missing from the online sessions. There were pros and cons to doing the class online, but it successfully provided a new entry point into Word-and-Sacrament ministry for nonchurched people.

When starting new ministries and activities to create additional entry points into the Word and Sacraments, it's important to assess what is of interest and appealing to the nonchurched people we are inviting. In some communities, meeting in homes instead of church buildings will be comfortable; in other communities, this may be uncomfortable. Some nonchurched people prefer working through a study on their own, while others are looking for more personal interaction and would prefer meeting in a group.

Some want to meet with the pastor to learn from someone whom they consider an expert and authority figure. Others are reluctant to engage with the pastor because of a past experience or feelings of inadequacy. The key to developing new entry points into Word-and-Sacrament ministry is to consider the context and the people we are inviting.

EFFECTIVE OUTREACH ALWAYS INVITES AND ENCOURAGES, NEVER FORCES OR MANIPULATES

This final aspect of effective outreach might be challenging for you because it reminds us that we need to be patient about inviting people into the Word-and-Sacrament ministry of our congregation. Because we know the good gifts that the Lord God gives through the Means of Grace and we care about the nonchurched people in our community, we are eager for people to enter into our Word-and-Sacrament ministry. But they may not be ready to make this step. We may need to spend more time and effort nurturing our relationships with them before they are open to an invitation into our Word-and-Sacrament ministry.

As a rule, people do not want to be pressured into a decision or commitment. If we invite people into our Word-and-Sacrament ministry before they are ready for such an invitation, they may feel that we are pressuring them to make a commitment. So how do we know when a person is ready for and open to an invitation to one of our entry points into Word and Sacrament? The answer to that question is found in the strength of the outreach relationship that we've developed with a person. The stronger the outreach relationship, the clearer the answer becomes.

There's another way that this calls for us to be patient. While we're nurturing relationships with nonchurched people, we need to watch the temptation to slip Word-and-Sacrament ministry into our relationship-building activities. We may have good intentions in adding a short devotion or a Bible reading to a relationship-building activity, but if it is not something that the nonchurched participants were expecting they may perceive it to be bait and switch.

No one likes to be the target of bait and switch. How would you feel if you were invited to a friend's home for dinner and before the meal he presented a multilevel marketing opportunity that he wanted you to join? It would be one thing if he had told you that he wanted to share a business opportunity when you came over for dinner. But it's bait and switch if he sprang it on you. Chances are that his doing so would damage your relationship with him. And that's what happens when we use bait and switch with non-churched people—it damages our relationships with them.

A co-worker once invited me to attend a musical in which he had a leading role. The performance was held at his non-Lutheran church, but it was billed as a musical, not a religious activity. Several colleagues also attended, including some who were nonchurched. The musical was fine, and our co-worker appreciated our support. Things went south when the church's pastor spoke after the musical. He said, "The music was nice, but the real reason we're here tonight is to talk about Jesus Christ and how you can make Him your Lord and Savior." He preached a short sermon and made an appeal for people to accept Jesus as their Savior (again, this was not a Lutheran church!). I watched my nonchurched co-workers grow increasingly uncomfortable—almost as uncomfortable as the co-worker who had invited us. We were victims of a bait and switch revealed by the pastor's comment "the real reason we're here tonight." It was embarrassing, uncomfortable, and ineffective.

Effective outreach calls for us to make invitations that are specific, appropriate, and appealing from the nonchurched person's point of view. We should never resort to bait and switch tactics and never try to force a person to accept our invitation by making her feel obligated in some way. Instead, we should make good invitations, be encouraging, and trust the Holy Spirit.

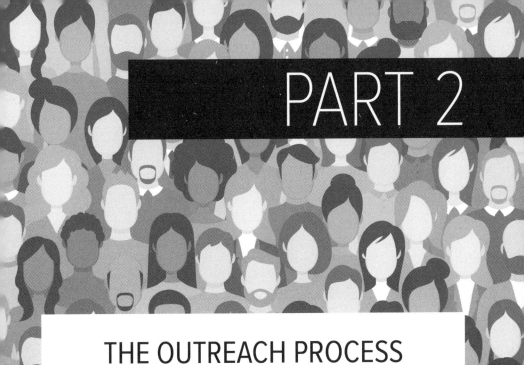

PART 2

THE OUTREACH PROCESS AND TOOLS

We've looked at the things that make outreach effective—the "what" and the "why" of outreach. Now let's turn our attention to the "how" of outreach. It's important to understand what makes for effective outreach. It's more important that we put it into practice. Actually, we're better off conducting outreach poorly than having the right answers about outreach but not actually doing outreach. It's even better to have good answers and put them into practice!

Keep in mind that there is not one right way to do outreach. The principles that we've already looked at as well as the process and tools that we are going to explore make up one good way to conduct outreach. They aren't meant to be an indelible blueprint for every congregation in every context. Instead, they are provided for you to assess and adapt to meet the challenges and opportunities of your congregation's unique context. Learn them, master them, and then mold them into the resources for effective outreach to the nonchurched people in your community.

CHAPTER 4

UNDERSTAND THE PERSPECTIVE OF NONCHURCHED PEOPLE

> To the weak I became weak, that I might win the weak. I have become all things to all people, that by all means I might save some. I do it all for the sake of the gospel, that I may share with them in its blessings. 1 CORINTHIANS 9:22–23

Have you ever passed by a building and wondered what goes on inside? Maybe it had an unusual name or housed a business that you weren't familiar with. You may have been curious, but you weren't curious enough to go into the building. If you live in a city or a suburb, there are probably buildings like this. And there are probably many other buildings that you pass by without even wondering what they are or what goes on inside of them.

This is what it is like for many of the nonchurched people who pass by your church's property. They may wonder what goes on inside or they may pass by without giving it any thought. Either way, they are unlikely to walk in the front door. Having a sign that welcomes people and invites them to come in isn't going to change that. From their perspective, your church is not a place for them.

There are many reasons why nonchurched people are unlikely to come into your church building. For some, it's too much of an unknown. They don't know what goes on inside a church and they are either too afraid, too apprehensive, or too indifferent to walk in the front door to find out. Other nonchurched people have

43

preconceived ideas about what goes on inside a church, and they don't want any part of it. Their ideas about churches are based on what they have seen through the media and entertainment industry—which often paint an undesirable picture of the Christian Church. There are other nonchurched people who do know what goes on inside but don't want anything to do with it. Some of them have had bad experiences in churches and can't deal with the hurts of the past. Others have drifted away and are too embarrassed to come back on their own. Some have consciously chosen to separate themselves from belonging to a church because they do not believe what that church teaches or practices. And some just think they know what the Christian Church is all about but have a flawed understanding of it.

Understanding the perspective of the nonchurched people we are trying to engage through outreach is complicated. Part of the complexity is that there is not a single point of view or attitude to address. There is always a mixture of perspectives among the people we are trying to reach out to. They range from being curious and open to invitations to being hostile and closed to anything that churches do. We should expect nonchurched people to have these various opinions and attitudes. And we should brace ourselves for being on the receiving end of criticism and hostility from nonchurched people who, for one reason or another, dislike churches.

When I was a church planter, I looked for opportunities to partner with organizations in our community to develop relationships and engage new people. One of those partnerships was with a group that raised funds for feeding the hungry but didn't have an outlet for distributing food to those in need. We were happy to provide a space for a food pantry and saw it as a great outreach activity. We set things up so members of our congregation could visit with the people waiting for food boxes, get to know them and their circumstances, and even pray with people who were open to it. Everything seemed to be going smoothly. To my surprise and dismay, the woman who led the fund-raising group informed me that her group would not allow our members to pray with the people coming for assistance and that she didn't even want church members involved in the food pantry—even though it was located on our property! While I knew that she was nonchurched, I didn't realize that she had a very negative view of churches. Our partnership ended quickly and the Lord provided other sources of funding to keep the food pantry going. In hindsight, I think we could have had a fruitful, long-term partnership if I had been more aware of and sensitive to the nonchurched woman's perspective of churches.

We can be surprised and dismayed when we find out what nonchurched people think about churches and, by extension, our congregation and her members. Sometimes we can be pleasantly surprised. There are people in our community who have a favorable view of churches and are open to invitations to church activities. Unfortunately, it seems that this is the case less and less in our culture. A more prominent view of the Christian Church in contemporary society is indifference. Most nonchurched people don't consider the Church to be relevant to their lives. They have filled their lives with many other things and don't see how the Church has any place in their busy and full lives. Of course, there are also nonchurched people who are hostile toward or angry with the Church.

Effective outreach begins with understanding how the nonchurched people in our community perceive the Church and its relevance to their lives. But there isn't just one perspective to consider. Our community is filled with people who have differing perspectives of the Church. If we address just one of those perspectives, we're going to exclude a lot of people from our outreach efforts. This is especially true if we take the easy way and focus on the people who have a positive view of the Church.

Considering and addressing the variety of perspectives about the Church held by the nonchurched people in our community requires us to put ourselves in their place. It calls for compassion and empathy—even for the people who are hostile toward the Church. Using the apostle Paul's experience as a guide, we aim to "become all things to all people" in order that they might hear the Good News of Jesus from us. It is challenging work, but it is not complex work. At each step of the outreach process, we assess what we are planning to do for outreach from the perspective of the nonchurched people we are seeking to reach with the Gospel. While we may not become "all things to all people," we can consider all people and all perspectives when planning and conducting our outreach efforts.

CHAPTER 5

THE OUTREACH PROCESS

> **What you have learned and received and heard and seen in me—practice these things, and the God of peace will be with you.** PHILIPPIANS 4:9

Outreach doesn't just happen. There may have been a time (though I doubt that there was) when we could have built a building, called a pastor, put up a sign, and then watched the church fill up with people from the community. But that is not the situation today. Effective outreach requires planning, and it calls for us to act intentionally.

When planning our outreach efforts, we do well to learn from the experiences of other congregations and to base our plans on principles of effective outreach. Those experiences and principles are captured in the outreach process that we'll be discussing in the remainder of this book. As we do, remember that this is a process, not a plan. We'll use the process to guide us through the steps that will help us create plans for effective outreach.

Keep in mind that this process is not the only way to plan and conduct outreach. Think of it as a newly constructed house. You've planned and anticipated the building of the house. You know that the floor plan, structure, and exterior are sound and set. You're confident that it is a good and functional house. But when you move in, you realize that it needs landscaping, furniture, window treatments, pictures, knickknacks, rugs, pillows, and more to make it your home. So first move into this process, then get comfortable with it, and finally make it your own.

There are four stages in the Outreach Process. Each stage leads to the next stage, though some people may skip a stage or two. Also, we may find that some of our outreach activities serve as a bridge between two stages and don't neatly fit into one stage or the other. The four stages of the Outreach Process are meant to help us plan intentional outreach. While we want to make good use of this process to plan and conduct effective outreach, we also don't want to fall into the trap of slavishly adhering to the stages.

Here is a diagram of the four stages of the Outreach Process:

These stages identify our plan for engaging nonchurched people and doing what we can do for them to become disciples of Jesus. Remember that people may skip a stage or two as they move through this process. On the other hand, not everyone who starts this process will complete it. As the diagram shows, those who do become disciples join the rest of our congregation in reaching out to other nonchurched people through the Outreach Process.

Let's take a close look at each of the four stages of the Outreach Process.

Stage 1 of the Outreach Process: Build Awareness

The starting point for effective outreach is to make people aware that our congregation exists and to communicate what we offer to the community. Whether our congregation is well established, a mission start, or somewhere in between, there are many people in our community who do not know who we are and why we exist. As hard as it is for us to believe, they may not even realize that we do exist.

When I travel to visit a congregation for a workshop or other activity, I often ask local people about the congregation. It's not unusual for a hotel receptionist, gas station attendant, or restaurant server to tell me that they don't know anything about the congregation. Once when I visited a congregation in a small town with fewer than 15,000 residents, I asked the motel front desk worker about the congregation. She didn't even know where it was. That surprised me because not only was the community small, but the congregation was prominently located on a main roadway. When I mentioned that it was located next to the local college campus, she said, "Oh, yeah. I drive past that church all the time."

The nonchurched people in our community are driving past our congregation all the time without giving any thought to our presence in the community. This means that passive methods of building awareness such as signs and banners don't have much of an impact. Rather than relying on them, we need to make use of more engaging forms of communication to gain the attention of the people we are seeking to inform about our congregation and our ministries and activities. Notice that there are two parts to building awareness: gaining people's attention and then informing them.

Informing people about the ministries and activities of our congregation isn't particularly difficult. The information about the ministry or activity can be incorporated into a well-crafted brochure or flyer, an appealing website that is easy to navigate, or a door hanger that is hand delivered. But even the most attractive printed material or engaging web page is of no value if we don't gain people's attention before we attempt to inform them.

Gaining people's attention can be challenging. Today, we are bombarded with information, so we ignore things that don't interest us. We recognize gimmicks that are used to break through the information overload and quickly dismiss them. If you've purchased a house or refinanced your mortgage, you're going to receive a lot of mail marked "Important: regarding your home loan" from companies trying to sell you a home warranty, life insurance, or other services. If you have a decent credit rating, you probably receive offers for "lowest rate" credit cards with "3 times the points" from credit card companies. What do you do with this junk mail? Despite the best efforts of the marketing people behind these offers, most of these mailings go straight from our mailbox to our home shredder.

That should be a lesson for us as we seek to gain people's attention. We can't resort to gimmicks, and we're not in a position to hire a professional marketing firm. So what can we do to cut through the noise? How do we gain the attention of people who, like us, are being bombarded with information every day? We start with understanding the perspectives of the nonchurched people we are reaching out to. Based on what is important to them and what they need or think they need, we offer something they are interested in because it meets their needs.

It is also important to decide the purpose of building awareness before making the effort to gain people's attention. How you go about gaining their attention will vary depending on what you want to inform them about once you have their attention. For example, you may want to increase awareness of your congregation's existence but don't have anything specific in mind. In this case, a billboard or ad at the local movie theater may be a good way to build awareness. This is known as "image advertising" to marketers because it makes an impression on the people who see the ad without overwhelming them with details. On the other hand, if you want people to attend a specific event like an Oktoberfest or living nativity, you'll need something informative that people can reference (e.g., a brochure, flyer, website page).

Build Awareness is an important first step in the Outreach Process—but it is only the first step. Marketing and advertising are part of outreach, but they are not outreach in and of themselves. We can use many different forms of marketing and advertising to build awareness of our congregation and the ministries and activities we conduct, but even the most impactful marketing and advertising won't make people disciples of Jesus.

Stage 2 of the Outreach Process: Create Connections

The goal of Build Awareness is to make the nonchurched people in our community aware of our congregation's ministries and activities with the hope and expectation that some of them will attend the events that we are promoting. It's gratifying when people outside our congregation attend an event or participate in an activity that we've publicized in the community. But we haven't created connections with the nonchurched people just because they have attended something we've sponsored. To actually create a connection, we need to establish some way of continuing contact with them after the event or activity.

Getting contact information and permission to use it from the people who come to our events and activities isn't especially complicated. It just requires us to be intentional about asking for it in a nonthreatening way. It also doesn't hurt to be a little creative about gathering it.

One of our outreach events for the congregation we started in Florida was a living nativity. Using a concept from another Lutheran church in our district, we put together a twelve scene journey through the life of Jesus. It was a gigantic undertaking for a young and small congregation. We publicized the event, recruited help from the community, and worked hard to build the sets, make the costumes, acquire props, and so forth. We were ready, but we weren't sure what to expect. To our delight, more than three hundred people from the community came to our event and heard the story of Jesus' life, death, and resurrection. Afterward, we realized that we didn't have a good way to follow up with the people who had attended. We hadn't created the connections we had hoped to create.

The next year, we made some adjustments to make sure we could continue contact with the people who attended. At the gathering point, we added a registration table with a scribe attending to a "census" scroll. Dressed as a Roman centurion, one of our members (a retired Marine Corps officer) greeted every guest with a loud and enthusiastic, "Halt! Caesar Augustus commands that you register for his census!" People quickly went to the registration table and provided the contact information. We had created connections—we had a way to continue contact with the people who attended our outreach event.

You don't need a Roman soldier to encourage people to share their contact information. You can gather it through enrollment in a class, drawings or raffles at community events, a "more information" form on your website, or other means. A friend of mine helped plan his congregation's "touch a truck" event. This event was designed to attract families with young children. They had different kinds of vehicles—from fire trucks to front loaders—on their campus for children to get close to, climb on, and sit in. Their way of creating connections was to offer free ice cream. How did free ice cream do this? By having people fill out a form to receive a coupon for the free ice cream. It was a simple, creative, and voluntary way of making sure that they were able to create connections through this community event.

There are a number of creative ways that we can request people's contact information at our outreach events, but we need to make sure that we are requesting the information, not insisting on it. People should not feel pressured to provide their contact information, Also, we should receive their permission to use the information to contact them with information about future events and activities. Once we have the information and permission, we need to use it wisely. We want to keep them informed of specific things, not just add them to our congregation's general email list. We need to be careful that we don't misuse the information by using it in ways for which we do not have permission. We also don't want to overuse it by sending too many announcements or making contact too frequently.

Stage 3 of the Outreach Process: Nurture Relationships

Most congregations are pretty good at the Build Awareness and Create Connections stages of the Outreach Process. They're even better at doing the things in the Make Disciples stage. But the

Nurture Relationships stage is often a challenging and neglected stage. This is where the process often breaks down.

Part of the reason that the Nurture Relationships stage is neglected by congregations is that churched people often don't see the need for starting and strengthening relationships with nonchurched people as part of outreach. Instead, they expect the nonchurched people to go from the Create Connections stage directly to the Make Disciples. In a way, there was a time when this was the case. In the past, congregations were often the centers of their communities. Many of the social events and special celebrations in the community were hosted by a local congregation. People didn't have to start by developing relationships as part of outreach because they already had relationships with nonchurched people in the community. Through the strength of those existing relationships, nonchurched people were open to invitations to come to worship services or attend a Bible study, the two most common entry points into Word-and-Sacrament ministry of a congregation.

Like many other aspects of our society, the place of the congregation as the center of community life has changed. Actually, the very nature of our community life has changed. In previous generations, much of life revolved around the relationships that people had with the others around them. Extended family members lived nearby, and friendships were forged early in life and lasted decades. Today we live in a very different society. Families are geographically scattered, and cousins are more likely to be near strangers than close friends. Most people, especially in urban and suburban settings, have only a few good friends—and those friendships tend to be short lived because of the transitory nature of our culture. Lifelong friendships are more the exception than the rule in our contemporary society.

Due to the individualistic nature of our society, the nonchurched people in our community live individual and isolated lives. Their small circles of friends are unlikely to include existing relationships with members of our congregation. Without those relationships, the nonchurched people that we connect with through our Create Connections outreach efforts are not open to our invitations to

Make Disciples activities. We need to create and develop relationships between the nonchurched people we connect with and members of our congregation.

When considering how to create and develop relationships with nonchurched people, we need to keep in mind that we are not talking about creating friendships, though it's possible that these relationships may become friendships. Instead, these relationships are more like those we develop with people who provide us products and services. In a word, we can call these relationships "professional" relationships. We have different kinds of professional relationships in our lives. They range from occasional interactions with people, such as the car salesperson we go back to years after buying a new vehicle, to more frequent interactions, such as the medical professionals who provide us with care on a routine basis.

There's nothing artificial about professional relationships just because they aren't friendships. We don't expect our automotive mechanic or the person who services our heating and air conditioning system to be our friend. But we do expect to be able to trust them to deal with us honestly and treat us fairly. If they don't, we'll look for a new mechanic or technician and start a new professional relationship. The bottom line is that professional relationships are centered in the products and services that people provide, and they are based on a trust that develops through experience. The same is true of the relationships that we are seeking to create and develop through our outreach efforts, which we will refer to as "outreach relationships." We provide services to the nonchurched people in our community through our ministries and activities that address their needs, and through those services we forge outreach relationships with them.

There are a few things to keep in mind while we are nurturing the outreach relationships that we create through our ministries and activities. First, as we've already discussed, outreach relationships are different from friendships. While we would like to see friendships grow out of the outreach relationships, many never become anything more than outreach relationships. That's perfectly okay because outreach relationships serve a different purpose than friendships do.

After I purchased a new vehicle from the local Ford dealer, I started getting birthday cards from Jake, the salesman who handled the transaction. Every year, I'd get a card from Jake. Was Jake eagerly celebrating my birthday year after year? Did I invite him to dinner to mark the occasion? Of course not. Jake was nurturing a professional relationship, not trying to forge a friendship with me. When the time came to purchase a new car, who did I contact at Brandon Ford? Jake was happy to sell me another car and to keep sending me birthday cards.

Another thing to consider about nurturing outreach relationships is that relationships are built over time through repeated interactions. We need to be mindful that the nonchurched people who come to our activities and events are venturing into something that is foreign to them. We need to provide additional ways for them to interact with the members of our congregation. The trust and respect of an outreach relationship is developed over time and through multiple interactions.

Too often we don't take the time or provide the opportunities for repeated interaction in our outreach efforts. Instead, we focus on getting nonchurched people to make the giant leap (in their minds) from attending an event to joining us in worship or Bible study. Earlier I likened this outreach approach to a first date proposal. It didn't matter how well that first date was going, the young lady was not likely to accept the impatient man's proposal and was probably scared off of a second date. Be patient. Take the time to enjoy the process of nurturing the relationship through the ongoing interactions that various events and activities provide.

There is one more thing to keep in mind when planning and conducting the activities and events that we use to nurture relationships. Whenever possible, use activities that provide repeated interactions with the same people. It's hard to foster relationships when contact takes place irregularly or a lot of time passes between interactions. A good example of an activity that provides repeated interactions with the same people is a class (e.g., parenting class, financial management class). A series of similar but standalone events (e.g., family movie night) is less effective because it doesn't provide consistent interaction between the same people from event to event. Be especially careful to avoid "one and done" activities when planning relationship-building outreach efforts, such as an annual Oktoberfest or spring fling. Events like these are good for creating connections but not for nurturing relationships—unless you're planning to propose on the first date!

Lastly, think through how you can start reaching nonchurched people with a few relationships in the congregation and then expand to many relationships. There are two reasons to use this few-to-many approach to nurturing relationships. First, we don't want to overwhelm the nonchurched people who participate in our relationship-building activities. It's better to start with one or two members, and then let them gradually introduce the nonchurched person to other members as the relationship develops.

The second reason is that structuring relationship building on the few-to-many model helps prevent concentrating our relationships with nonchurched people to a small group of our members. Too often we let the people in the congregation who are gifted in relationship building nurture all the relationships we create with nonchurched people. In some congregations, the pastor, whether he is gifted in relationship building or not, is the default relationship person in the congregation. While this may be comfortable for members who aren't especially gifted in relationship building, it is ineffective because the person or persons who are building relationships have a limited capacity for new relationships. It also keeps us from expanding relationships with members of the congregation through the few-to-many approach. In some congregations, all those relationships are centered in one person—usually the pastor.

The danger is that these relationships end when the congregation member is no longer part of the congregation. This is especially the case when a pastor leaves the congregation through a new call, retirement, or death. I previously mentioned how in my first call as a pastor I served a congregation whose pastor of more than twenty years had passed away while serving them. In addition to the shock and grief that the active members were experiencing, many people had stopped attending worship services and Bible study. When I contacted the people who had disappeared after the pastor's death, I heard a common response: "I just can't bring myself to come back. There are too many memories of Pastor Schultz there." Pastor Schultz (not his real name) was great at relationship building, but many of the relationships he created and nurtured with nonchurched people never went beyond him. When he died, so did the connection between these people and the congregation.

To avoid the trap of leaving relationship building to the pastor and the few members who are naturally good at it, we need to equip other members of the congregation with skills and resources for relationship building. Not everyone in the congregation is going to be willing to be trained on how to start and develop outreach relationships with nonchurched people. However, everyone in the congregation should receive training on what outreach relationships are and how they are important for effective outreach. It's also helpful for all members to be aware of the people who have been trained as relationship builders so they can connect nonchurched people with the fully trained members at outreach activities and events.

Stage 4 of the Outreach Process: Make Disciples

Seeing people become disciples of Jesus is the desired outcome of our outreach efforts. The things we do through the Build Awareness, Create Connections, and Nurture Relationships stages are important elements of effective outreach, but they do not and cannot make someone a disciple. Only the Holy Spirit working through the Means of Grace (i.e., God's Word and His Sacraments) makes disciples. Our outreach efforts are meant to bring the Means of Grace to people and bring people the Means of Grace.

Not only do we want to share the Means of Grace with people but we also want to do so in ways that are faithful to God's Word. The same Holy Spirit who works faith through the Means of Grace has called us to make use of God's Word and Sacraments in ways that are right and good. To that end, we don't set up loudspeakers outside the church building and blast the reading of the Bible to people passing by. We also wouldn't dream of renting a fire truck for the Fourth of July parade and hosing people down in the name of the Father, Son, and Holy Spirit. We want to make proper use of these precious treasures.

We also want to share the Means of Grace in ways that are of interest to the nonchurched people we would like to become disciples through our outreach efforts. In other words, we want to show people how God's Word and Sacraments are relevant to their lives. That's very different than trying to make God's Word and Sacraments relevant to nonchurched people—which is impossible for us to do because they are already relevant. Our role in sharing the Means of Grace with people is to invite them into the Word-and-Sacrament ministry of our congregation through an entry point that is of interest and is appealing to them.

How do we know which Word-and-Sacrament entry point is of interest to a particular nonchurched person? We could flood her with invitations to every entry point and see which one she finds interesting. But that approach is just as likely to overwhelm her and drive her away. A better way would be to get to know her through an outreach relationship and invite her to something that would be of interest to her based on what you've learned about her and her life.

One example of how this has worked in my parish ministry experience is the Young Families Home Group. The congregations I served in Florida routinely received requests from nonchurched parents to have their children baptized. In most cases, the parents were new parents who were dechurched, had moved to Florida from the Midwest, and were anticipating a visit from their baby's grandparents. Even though they had drifted away from the Church, they still considered Baptism to be important for their children—or at least to their parents' grandchildren.

In the past, the congregation had baptized the children, added the family to the cradle role mailing list, and hoped for the best. Not surprisingly, few of those families became active in the congregation, which is a nice way of saying that they got what they wanted and we never saw them again. To engage the nonchurched parents of these newly baptized children, we started the Young

Families Home Group. The group met twice a month, one time for a Bible study called "Parents in the Bible" and one time for a social activity. People were free to come to either or both meetings. Through the Young Families Home Group, relationships were formed and strengthened—so much so that we had to start a Growing Families Home Group as the children got older. Through those relationships, parents who might otherwise have "had the kid done" (yes, that is how some actually said it) and disappeared joined us in the study of God's Word and became active disciples of Jesus Christ.

The example of the Young Families Home Group reminds us that while the desired outcome of our outreach efforts takes place in the Make Disciples phase of the Outreach Process, each phase of the process is designed to help us help nonchurched people enter into the Word-and-Sacrament ministry of our congregation where the Holy Spirit works faith—makes disciples—when and where He wills.

Before leaving the topic of the Means of Grace being of interest to nonchurched people, I need to address a misunderstanding about outreach, worship, and nonchurched people. The biggest misconception among churched people about outreach is the idea that we should change or need to change our worship style to attract nonchurched people to our congregation. From what I've learned about nonchurched people, I seriously doubt that they are sitting at home thinking to themselves that they would start worshiping at your congregation if you would offer a different style of worship.

Unlike churched people, nonchurched people, especially unchurched people, don't have a preference about worship style. In my experience, nonchurched people expect worship services to be something different than their experiences in everyday life. They aren't coming to a worship service because we offer one type of service or another. They are coming because we have made a connection, nurtured an outreach relationship, and invited them to enter into the Word-and-Sacrament ministry of our congregation in a way that is of interest to them.

Worship style is not a concern of the nonchurched. Changing worship style is not an effective way of conducting outreach. It may attract churched people who have a preference, but it will not interest the nonchurched people we are trying to reach.

CHAPTER 6

THE OUTREACH FUNNEL

> **When the young man heard this he went away sorrowful, for he had great possessions.** MATTHEW 19:22

Wouldn't it be great if every person who learned about our congregation and the things that we are doing through our Build Awareness outreach efforts would become a disciple of Jesus? Or if not all those people, perhaps all the people who attended our Create Connections events and activities? Well, how about at least everyone we get to know through our ongoing Nurture Relationships activities? We know that not everyone we engage through our outreach efforts will end up becoming a disciple of Jesus. But we don't know which people will and which people won't. Keeping that in mind, we want to treat every person whom we engage through our outreach efforts as a potential disciple and to do what we can to facilitate their journey through the Outreach Process. At the same time, we want to be realistic about the attrition that is likely to take place as we work with people through the Outreach Process so we don't become disillusioned or discouraged.

A good way to visualize the reality that each phase of the Outreach Process involves a decreasing number of people is a graphic called the Outreach Funnel. The Outreach Funnel is based on a tool—the sales funnel—widely used in the secular world to train people in sales and marketing. The idea behind the sales funnel is that each sale of a product or service is the result of many preceding actions involving many more contacts, presentations, negotiations, and so on. My brother-in-law uses the

The Traditional Sales Funnel

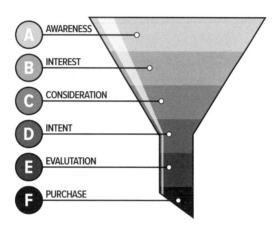

A — AWARENESS
B — INTEREST
C — CONSIDERATION
D — INTENT
E — EVALUTATION
F — PURCHASE

sales funnel in his insurance business. To promote his business, he was considering using a company that mails out packets of coupons. His goal was to establish five new clients. To do this, he estimated that the coupons needed to reach several thousand homes to generate a few hundred responses. From those few hundred responses, he expected that a few dozen people would actually meet with him. If he was right and he was able to meet with a few dozen interested people, he would probably meet his goal of gaining five new clients.

The numbers vary based on the product or service being promoted, the market size, the capacity of the business, and other factors, but the principle of the sales funnel remains the same. It starts with a large number of people who might be interested in what you are offering and narrows down to a few interested and committed people. The sales funnel is a tool that we can make use of as a First Article gift—that is, a resource that God has provided as part of His creation that is available to all people regardless of faith. As with other First Article gifts (music, technology, transportation, government), we want to make faithful use of the sales funnel insofar as it helps us carry out the work that the Lord has entrusted to us. To that end, the Outreach Funnel makes use of the principles of the sales funnel and applies them to making disciples through the Outreach Process.

The Outreach Funnel does make one important revision to the sales funnel. The sales funnel is presented in the way that one would expect to see a funnel positioned. It has the large opening of the funnel on the top and the small opening on the bottom. We can relate well to that image because that is how we use actual funnels. Everything that goes into the top of the funnel comes out the bottom. However, that's not the case in sales and marketing and it is not the case in outreach. While the image of a funnel does a good job of depicting the narrowing that takes place throughout the Outreach Process, if it is left in its upright position it is misleading. Not everyone who enters the funnel through our outreach efforts will come out a disciple of Jesus. To show that more clearly, the Outreach Funnel is pictured on its side. The sideways funnel still shows the narrowing down that takes place through the Outreach Process, and it shows that we need to take action to help people move through the funnel.

Outreach Funnel

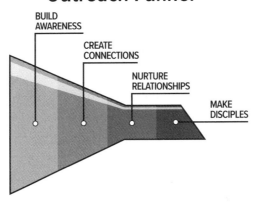

Imagine putting something in a sideways funnel. If you simply place it in the funnel, it will drop to the bottom and come back out. If you want it to go through the funnel, you'll need to do something to move it from the large part to the narrow part. In the same way, we need to act intentionally to help people move through the Outreach Funnel.

The Outreach Funnel has four parts. Each part represents a stage of the Outreach Process, and the progression through the funnel follows the sequence of the Outreach Process. The widest part of the Outreach Funnel is the Build Awareness stage of the process. It shows that we will engage the greatest number of people through our advertising and marketing. It also reminds us that most of the people we engage through our Build Awareness activities will not continue their interaction with us into the next stage of the Outreach Funnel, which is Create Connections. That narrowing down of the number of people we are engaging continues in the Create Connections stage. We should expect that many of the nonchurched people from our community who attend an activity or event will not provide us with the information we need to continue contact or will ignore our efforts to continue contact with them (e.g., they will unsubscribe from our email list). Using the Outreach Funnel as a visual guide helps us keep this reality in mind as we plan and carry out our outreach efforts.

The third section of the Outreach Funnel is best pictured as a narrow and long segment of the funnel to convey that the Nurture Relationships stage of the Outreach Process involves fewer people over longer periods of time. Most of this takes place during the Build Awareness and Create Connections stages. There is much less narrowing in the Nurture Relationships stage but much more time involved. You may find that you can plan and conduct an outreach event and get through the Build Awareness and Create Connections stages in a few weeks but then spend months engaging the nonchurched people who enter the Nurture Relationships stage before they are open to being invited and included in the Word-and-Sacrament ministry of our congregation.

The fourth section of the Outreach Funnel is also shown as a narrow part of the funnel because the few people who do end up entering the Word-and-Sacrament ministry of our congregation through our outreach efforts tend to remain active in it. One reason that there isn't much narrowing in this stage is that people enter it on the strength of the relationships that have been fostered in the Nurture Relationships stage. The greater reason is that once people enter in the Word-and-Sacrament ministry of our congregation, they realize that it meets the greatest unmet need that they have. That's not to say that there won't be some people who won't drop out after participating in our Word-and-Sacrament ministry. Remember, the Holy Spirit works faith when and where He wills. Not everyone who enters the Make Disciples phase of the Outreach Process will become a disciple of Jesus. We can do our work of planting and watering through our outreach efforts to Build Awareness, Create Connections, Nurture Relationships, and Make Disciples. It's up to the Holy Spirit to do His work to give the growth that we desire and pray for.

The Outreach Process and the Outreach Funnel are tools to help us plan and conduct outreach activities. The actual plan for our outreach is captured in another tool for effective outreach called the Outreach Pathway.

CHAPTER 7

OUTREACH PATHWAYS

> In the path of righteousness is life, and in its pathway there is no death. PROVERBS 12:28

What Is an Outreach Pathway?

An Outreach Pathway is a visual plan for guiding us. Think of an Outreach Pathway as a road map for outreach. It captures and conveys the steps that we plan to take to guide nonchurched people from a point of connection with our congregation into relationship-building activities with our members and then into the Word-and-Sacrament ministry of our congregation.

Of course, not all road maps are created equal. Over the years, I've done my share of driving across the country. Many of those trips were taken before we had GPS and online mapping services. Actually, many of those trips predated the public use of GPS satellites and the existence of the internet! To get to where we were going, we relied on paper maps. We had to find our own routes, using those maps and our best guesses about which roads to take. At one time, an auto club provided an upgrade by creating a route map for us. These personalized maps gave us one route to our destination with the best information available at the time of their printing. In a very real way, this is how many congregations approach outreach. They leave it to the nonchurched people to find their own way into the congregation. If the congregation has a "map," it is likely to provide only one way for to engage nonchurched people: the worship service.

Taking a trip today is very different than it was when I made my first cross-country drive from Illinois to Williams AFB in Arizona in 1977. Today I can rely on GPS. This is so reliable (most of the time) that I don't have to plan my drive in any detail. Being a cautious person, and distrusting devices to some degree, I still plan my trip. But I don't use paper maps or the auto club. Instead, I use online mapping tools that provide me with multiple options for my drive. I can set parameters, check for construction zones, avoid toll roads, explore side trips, and see all the options for getting to my destination. This is what Outreach Pathways seek to do to help us help nonchurched people move through the Outreach Process.

Outreach Pathways

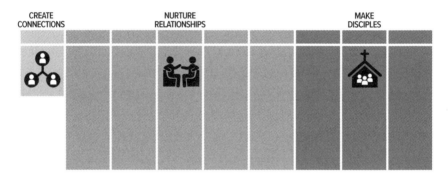

To visualize the relationship between the Outreach Funnel and an Outreach Pathway, picture a three-dimensional Outreach Funnel made up of the Create Connections, Nurture Relationships, and Make Disciples phases of the Outreach Process. (The Build Awareness phase is not part of the Outreach Pathway.) Now, slice the Outreach Funnel horizontally on one side, roll it open, and flatten it. The phases of the Outreach Funnel form the sections of the Outreach Pathway, starting with Create Connections. Vertical lines are added to the Nurture Relationships and Make Disciples phases to create columns. Each of those columns—swim lanes—show the activities that a single person is responsible for, so there is a place at the top of each column to add the name of the responsible person. Using this format, we are ready to create Outreach Pathways.

One thing to keep in mind when creating an Outreach Pathway is that it is a plan for one potential path for a nonchurched person to take through the Outreach Process. Because there are many different nonchurched people whom we will engage through our outreach activities, and there may be multiple ways for nonchurched people to move through the Outreach Process, there is not a single Outreach Pathway for a congregation. Instead, we need to create and use many Outreach Pathways, with each one addressing a specific kind of nonchurched person and a specific path through the Outreach Funnel.

Another thing to be mindful of when creating and using Outreach Pathways is that they are plans. Plans are useful for getting organized, communicating actions, assigning responsibilities, and thinking through various possibilities, but they are likely to change when they are put into practice. Use Outreach Pathways to create plans for effective outreach, and make good use of them when guiding people through the Outreach Funnel, but don't let the plan become more important than the desired outcome. If a nonchurched person wants to go directly from Create Connections to Make Disciples, don't insist that he has to follow your Outreach Pathway.

What Makes for an Effective Outreach Pathway?

An effective Outreach Pathway is one that helps us help nonchurched people progress through the Outreach Funnel. The Outreach Pathway is a tool for our congregation. While it's not a secret, it isn't something that we would share with the nonchurched people we are seeking to engage through our outreach efforts. But we do want to share it with the members of our congregation so that they are aware of the outreach activities that we are undertaking and how they relate to all our ministries and activities.

The most important characteristic of an effective Outreach Pathway is simplicity. Keeping a pathway simple will help it better communicate what we are planning to do and who is responsible for carrying it out. It's far better to have multiple simple Outreach Pathways for a specific type of nonchurched person than to have a single Outreach Pathway that tries to capture all the possible ways that a person may progress through the Outreach Funnel. Not only will simple Outreach Pathways do a better job of communicating our outreach plans within the congregation, but they will also be much easier to modify to keep our outreach efforts on track and we will be better able to make use of them for creating pathways for other types of nonchurched people.

Simplicity is the most important characteristic of an effective Outreach Pathway, but it isn't the only one. Let's take a brief look at a few additional characteristics of effective Outreach Pathways. (We'll explore these and additional characteristics further in Chapter 3).

AN EFFECTIVE OUTREACH PATHWAY FOCUSES ON ONE AND ONLY ONE SPECIFIC TYPE OF NONCHURCHED PERSON

Nonchurched people have differing interests, preferences, experiences, unmet needs, and so forth. It's impossible for a single Outreach Pathway to address all the factors that affect nonchurched people. In fact, the most effective Outreach Pathways will be those that are narrowly focused on a single type of nonchurched person.

Imagine going to a paint or hardware store to buy blue paint. You ask for blue paint. A good worker would need to ask lots of questions before she could sell you the paint. What type of paint to you need? How many gallons? Which of the four thousand shades of blue do you prefer? Obviously, just asking for blue paint isn't specific enough for the worker to fill your order.

When we seek to engage nonchurched people, we need to be specific about what kind of nonchurched people we are trying to reach—which of the four thousand types of nonchurched people are specifically seeking to engage through a particular outreach effort? Planning and using an Outreach Pathway works best when we clearly and specifically define the type of nonchurched people. The most effective Outreach Pathways are the most focused ones.

AN EFFECTIVE OUTREACH PATHWAY PROVIDES AN UNBROKEN SEQUENCE OF ACTIVITIES FROM CREATE CONNECTIONS TO NURTURE RELATIONSHIPS TO MAKE DISCIPLES

The main purpose of the Outreach Pathway is to capture and communicate what we are planning to do to help a specific type of nonchurched person to progress through the stages of the Outreach Process. It is a road map through the Outreach Funnel to help us help nonchurched people move from a connection through relationship building and into the Word-and-Sacrament ministry of our congregation. To do this, the Outreach Pathway needs to provide an unbroken, logical sequence of activities through each phase of the Outreach Process.

The unbroken, logical sequence of activities of the Outreach Pathway not only produces a plan for outreach but also provides us with a way to check the plan for obstacles and gaps. Obstacles are things that get in the way of a nonchurched person progressing through the Outreach Process and prevent him from moving from one phase to the next. Gaps are things that are missing in the flow of the Outreach Pathway that result in nonchurched people dropping out of the Outreach Process, that is, falling out of the Outreach Funnel. The good news about obstacles and gaps is that they can be fixed. The bad news is that new obstacles and gaps are likely to emerge over time. The Outreach Pathway is a good tool for mitigating obstacles and gaps when planning outreach efforts and a good tool for identifying and resolving new ones when they creep up.

An example of an obstacle would be having activities planned without having a person responsible for making sure that the activity gets done. This obstacle would show up on the Outreach Pathway as a blank box at the top of a swim lane where the responsibility for activities is documented. Gaps show up when an activity on the Outreach Pathway has no activity feeding into it or no activity following it. Gaps can easily be identified on the Outreach Pathway by following the lines that show the pathway's flow. An effective pathway has an unbroken flow of outreach activities through the stages of the Outreach Process without obstacles or gaps.

An Effective Outreach Pathway Demonstrates Who Ensures What at Each Stage of the Outreach Process

An Outreach Pathway not only shows what we are doing to engage a specific type of nonchurched person but it also shows who is responsible for making sure that the outreach activities take place as planned. By organizing the Outreach Pathway into columns or swim lanes, we have a simple and understandable tool for assigning responsibility for specific activities to specific people. At the top of each swim lane, there is a box for the name of the person responsible.

It's important to enter only one name at the top of the swim lane. Assigning multiple people the responsibility for a swim lane's activities will create confusion and create a gap in the pathway. If you need more room to keep the responsibility assignments clear, you can add another swim lane to the Outreach Pathway. Also make sure that you assign responsibility for a swim lane to a person and not to a board, committee, or team. Having a single and specific person responsible for the activities in a swim lane will minimize obstacles and gaps.

Keep in mind that being responsible for a swim lane is not the same as having to do the activities in that lane. The responsible person may do the activity herself, work with others to do the work, or delegate the work to other people altogether. However she chooses to make sure that the work is done, she remains responsible for the work. Keeping responsibility assignments clear helps to avoid obstacles and gaps and makes for an effective Outreach Pathway.

Outreach Pathways are the practical application of the Outreach Process and Outreach Funnel. Putting together simple, straightforward, and understandable pathways is the key to effective outreach. Let's look at what it takes to create useful and beneficial Outreach Pathways.

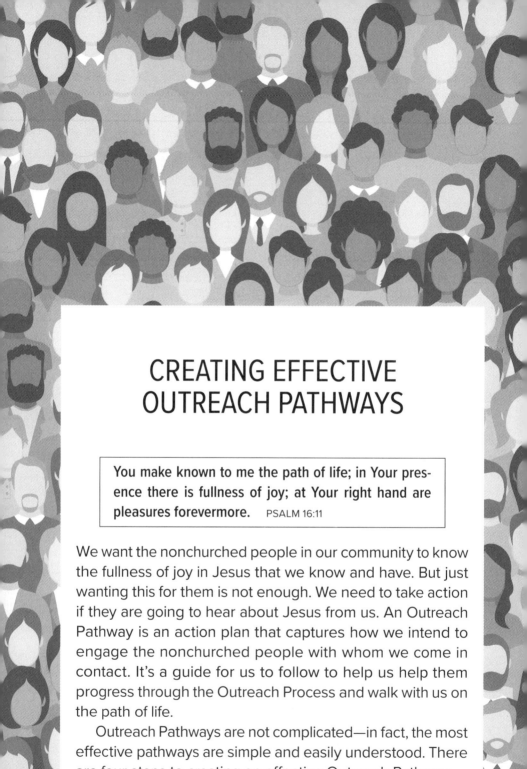

CREATING EFFECTIVE OUTREACH PATHWAYS

> You make known to me the path of life; in Your presence there is fullness of joy; at Your right hand are pleasures forevermore.   PSALM 16:11

We want the nonchurched people in our community to know the fullness of joy in Jesus that we know and have. But just wanting this for them is not enough. We need to take action if they are going to hear about Jesus from us. An Outreach Pathway is an action plan that captures how we intend to engage the nonchurched people with whom we come in contact. It's a guide for us to follow to help us help them progress through the Outreach Process and walk with us on the path of life.

Outreach Pathways are not complicated—in fact, the most effective pathways are simple and easily understood. There are four steps to creating an effective Outreach Pathway

PART 3

1. Use **SNAIL** to focus on a **WHOM**

2. Select a Pathway Conduit

3. Identify and Evaluate Pathway Activities

4. Arrange and Capture the Outreach Pathway

1 Use SNAIL to Focus on a WHOM	2 Select a Pathway Conduit	3 Identify and Evaluate Pathway Activities	4 Arrange and Capture the Outreach Pathway

As we look at each of these steps, keep in mind that we are creating a plan for engaging nonchurched people in our community. Like other plans, the Outreach Pathways we create need to be reviewed and revised to address changing circumstances and to make improvements based on our experiences. A plan is a tool to guide us in effective outreach, not something to lock us into one specific way of doing things. Like any other plan, an Outreach Pathway is a wonderful servant. However, it makes for a terrible master.

CHAPTER 8

Creating Effective Outreach Pathways

STEP 1: USE SNAIL TO FOCUS ON A WHOM

The outreach question people ask me most frequently is, "How do we reach young people?" That's a good question, but it isn't a question that can be answered without additional questions. "Young people" includes a wide variety of people. We need to define a more specific type of "young person" before we start planning our outreach efforts. We should ask questions like, "What age range of young people are we seeking to engage?" and "Are we trying to engage young people who are single or young couples?" and "Do we want to engage young people with children or without children?" and "Are we trying to reach college students or young people who are already working in their occupations?" There are more questions that we can and should ask before planning an Outreach Pathway for reaching young people. The answer to the question "How do we reach young people?" begins with narrowing the type of young person we are seeking to engage to a specific type of young person.

What's true for reaching young people is true for outreach to any type of nonchurched people. To be effective, we need to narrow the people we are seeking to engage through our outreach efforts. Limiting an Outreach Pathway to a single and specific type of people will help us produce focused, clear, and useful Outreach Pathways. The specific type of person that we want to focus on when planning our outreach efforts is called a WHOM, which stands for "Who Has Our Mission focus." Narrowing the variety of nonchurched people in our community to a WHOM is the first step in creating effective pathways. This effort can be summed up with the acronym SNAIL (Specific, Nonchurched, Accessible, Interested, and Local).

SNAIL—SPECIFIC

One of the most common mistakes that congregations make when planning their outreach efforts is failing to focus on a specific type of nonchurched people for a particular outreach activity. Because our communities are made up of many kinds of people with differing interests and needs, a general approach to outreach is unlikely to have much of an impact. While we may want to engage all the people in our community through our outreach efforts, there is not a universal outreach activity that will reach every kind of nonchurched person in our community. We need to plan outreach as a number of small-scale outreach efforts focused on specific types of nonchurched people rather than as a large-scale, one-size-fits-all outreach program.

There isn't a hard and fast rule about how specific we should get when we are planning our outreach efforts. Generally, the degree to which you need to narrow down the type of person will be driven by the outreach activities you are planning in the pathway. This means that you may have to adjust how specific you are getting as you progress through creating an Outreach Pathway. Some of the factors you should consider include the demographics of your community, the diversity of the type of people you are seeking to engage, and the capabilities of your congregation.

Demographics play an important role in narrowing down the type of nonchurched people to focus on in your outreach efforts because they help identify the types of people in your community and indicate the number of people in each type. For example, a congregation in a community with a large number of young families will get more specific when narrowing down the type of young family they want to engage than a congregation in a community with few young families. When planning outreach to young families, demographics will also provide you with insights into the diversity within that group. For example, demographics will identify the young families by ethnicity, income levels, religious affiliation, education, how long they've lived in the community, the amount of debt they have, and a host of other attributes. This information is helpful in determining how specific you should get when planning outreach to young families. It's also useful for developing ideas for outreach activities that would be of interest to the people you're reaching out to.

You'll probably find that there are not large numbers in some of the types of people that you'd like to engage. As you get specific, you may realize that there aren't enough nonchurched people in your community to focus your outreach efforts on a specific group of people. When you run into this situation, don't give up on reaching out to the people you've identified. Instead, use a different basis for getting specific. Look for some common characteristics that will help you focus on a type of person that is more plentiful in your community. For example, when we developed the Young Families Home Group, we were reaching out to different kinds of young families. Some were blended families that included stepparents. Others were traditional families. Some had extended family nearby, but most were far away from grandparents and cousins. Some had older children, while others only had pre-kindergarten children. There were many ways in which these families were different and had different needs and interests. We could have gotten very specific about the type of young families that we wanted to reach out to, but we couldn't address all these different things. Instead, we got specific by identifying common needs and interests among the different types of young families. We decided to focus on addressing the challenges of parenting young children. That focus was specific enough to identify the families that we were aiming to reach without splintering the group into segments that were too small to effectively serve.

As you work through how specific to get with a particular type of nonchurched people, you may find it helpful to create a profile of a person to picture. For example, you could describe a young family in your community as a couple who met during college, got married after graduating, moved into your community six years ago to start their careers, have a three-year-old boy and a six-month-old daughter, and the wife now stays at home to care for their children. A detailed profile like this will guide you in developing effective pathways for reaching young families. You may even find it helpful to give names to the characters you create in your profile to make them seem more real when you are creating and evaluating pathways. Instead of asking "What would be of interest to the wife in this family?" you would ask, "Why would Susan be interested in this activity?"

Make sure that you take your congregation's capabilities into consideration when getting specific about the people you want to reach. You may want to create outreach activities that are of interest to and are appealing to each different kind of young family in your community, but you may not have the people, money, space, or other resources for such a wide range of activities. Make an inventory of what the Lord has invested in your congregation, and plan how specific you can be with the resources you have.

SNAIL—NONCHURCHED

It should go without saying that an effective Outreach Pathway is going to be focused on engaging nonchurched people. But it needs to be said for two reasons. First, your outreach efforts may attract and engage people who are already active in another Christian congregation. Churched people in your community have some of the same unmet needs as nonchurched people in your community. When you offer something that addresses an unmet need, people—churched and nonchurched—will be interested. You should expect this and plan accordingly. While the churched people may not be the intended objects of your outreach efforts, they are people who need the care and compassion of Christ. You may decide to include them if you have the capacity to do so without hindering your efforts to engage nonchurched people. Just remember, serving churched people is not outreach.

The second reason to highlight that effective Outreach Pathways are focused on nonchurched people is that there are different kinds of nonchurched people that we need to consider when planning outreach. We've already discussed the major division of nonchurched into dechurched (once had a connection to a Christian church but no longer does) and unchurched (never had a connection to a Christian church). But that distinction is only the starting point. Further clarification of the types of nonchurched people we are seeking to engage is an important part of planning.

Think about the dechurched people you know. How many of them stopped coming to worship and then disappeared over a long period of inactivity by simply drifting away? How many left a church in anger over a decision by leadership or a change in practice? How many were hurt in some way by a leader or another member and have stayed away because they are still hurting? How many left because they were worn out by too many demands or expectations? There are many reasons that people leave churches. When you are planning an Outreach Pathway, you should put yourself in the shoes of the different kinds of dechurched people and consider how they might perceive things based on their previous experiences in churches.

There is a positive side to reaching out to dechurched people. Many of the people who have lost their connection to a church are open to invitations to come back. They know that they are missing something important in their lives. They are unlikely to take the initiative to come back on their own, but they are responsive to our outreach efforts. Don't overlook this important dimension to reaching out to dechurched people in your community.

One of the best ways to begin intentional outreach to dechurched people is to focus on the dechurched people who used to be connected to your congregation. This would include long-term inactive members, people who used to attend worship and Bible study but never became official members, people who were once active as volunteers in one of your human care ministries, and students who graduated from your day school. The Outreach

Pathways would look different for each of these groups of people, but they would all make use of the common strength of building on an established, though dormant, relationship.

Planning outreach to unchurched people has its own set of challenges. Like dechurched people, there are many kinds of unchurched people. Some unchurched people are or have been active in a non-Christian religion such as Islam, Judaism, or Hinduism. Others are involved in religious organizations that claim to be Christian churches but are not, such as the Church of Jesus Christ of Latter-day Saints (Mormons) and the Jehovah's Witnesses. Most unchurched people have no religious affiliation—though they may identify themselves as Christians because of their moral values, historical family ties to Christianity, or an understanding of Christianity as the default religion of Americans.

Such a wide variety of religious perspectives among the unchurched people in your community needs to be considered when focusing your outreach efforts to a specific group of people. If you don't think through how to engage specific types of unchurched people, you may end up offending or alienating people. What might be welcomed by one type of unchurched people may close the doors for outreach with another type. Don't treat all unchurched people the same when planning your outreach efforts.

SNAIL—ACCESSIBLE

In simple terms, *outreach* means "reaching out." It would be pointless to reach out to people whom you cannot reach. Instead, you want to focus your outreach efforts on people you can reach—that is, people who are accessible to you. While we may want to reach out to every person in our community, some are not accessible to us because of barriers or obstacles that we cannot overcome.

One obstacle that may make people inaccessible to us is language. If nonchurched people in our community do not speak any English and none of our members speak their language, those people are not accessible to us. We may be able to do some things to make those people accessible, but we may find that despite our best efforts they remain inaccessible to us. For example, we may offer English language courses to help overcome the language barrier only to discover that the people we are trying to make more accessible to us have no interest in learning English.

Another barrier is culture. I remember speaking with an African immigrant pastor about outreach in his community. Most of the nonchurched people in that community were Muslims. He explained that the Muslims were not permitted by their leaders to interact with Christians. This prohibition was strictly enforced by the leaders and other members of the community, which created a cultural barrier that made the people inaccessible to his congregation.

While it can be frustrating to know that there are inaccessible people in your community who don't know Jesus, it is also instructive. Just as the Holy Spirit made the people of Asia Minor inaccessible to the apostle Paul, He made the people of Macedonia accessible (see Acts 16:6–10). There may be inaccessible nonchurched people in your community, but there are definitely nonchurched people in your community who are accessible to you. Focus your outreach efforts on the people who are currently accessible while continuing to pray that the Holy Spirit will open doors for the Gospel for those who are currently inaccessible.

SNAIL—INTERESTED

When thinking about a type of nonchurched person to reach out to, ask yourself who might be interested in what your congregation has to offer. Keep in mind that being interested is different than having a need. We know that all nonchurched people need God's grace and need faith in Jesus for life and salvation. They need Christ's forgiveness and love. But that doesn't mean that they are interested in those things.

It's also important to be mindful that we can't offer some things that people would be interested in because we don't have the capacity to offer them or because they fall outside our mission and purpose as a congregation. For example, nonchurched people in our community may be interested in learning how to win at casino games like blackjack and craps. But even if we had members who were gaming experts and willing to teach people how to win at these games, teaching people how to gamble conflicts with our congregation's purpose and mission.

Knowing the shape of your community is a good starting point for determining who might be interested in what your congregation is offering or could offer. After you have identified what is of interest to the nonchurched people in your community in general, you can identify which specific types of people in your community would be interested in your ministries and activities. Look around and see what people are doing. Do you see a lot of people riding bicycles? Maybe they'd be interested in a cycling club. Does your community have several golf courses? If so, there are probably nonchurched people who would be interested in something related to golfing. Are the neighborhood parks filled with parents watching their young children on the playground? Those parents may be interested in activities like a parenting class or a support group for themselves or a play group for their children.

As you work to narrow the focus of your outreach efforts to a specific type of person, don't start planning the activities yet. We'll do that in the third step of creating effective Outreach Pathways. Instead, picture the nonchurched people in your community and their interests rather than the things you might do to respond to their interests.

SNAIL—LOCAL

As we discussed earlier, outreach is always local. It follows then that the people we are seeking to engage through our outreach efforts are local people, that is, people who live near our congregation. When you are planning outreach for specific types of people, make sure you are considering the people who make up the neighborhood around your congregation. That seems rather straightforward, but it can be challenging, especially when the members of your congregation don't know the people in your neighborhood. This is a real challenge for congregations that I call "commuter churches."

A commuter church is a congregation that has a significant number of members who don't live near the church. On any given

Sunday, people will drive thirty, forty, fifty or more miles to attend that congregation's worship service, often passing other congregations as they commute. There are good reasons to commute a long distance to church. For example, there may not be another faithful pastor and congregation any closer. There are also some not-so-good reasons to commute to a congregation in another community that have to do with selfish choices. In any case, outreach is more challenging for a commuter church because the members are disconnected from the nonchurched people in the neighborhood surrounding the church.

I often find commuter churches in urban settings. The people who attend the church drive in from the suburbs on Sunday morning, unlock the building and grounds, conduct services for the members, and then lock up and go home. The properties are often fenced off for security, and there aren't church activities during the week, with the possible exception of midweek services during Advent and Lent, because it is so far away from the members' homes. Many of the members continue to attend this church because they have deep roots in the congregation, including family history. I understand that connection, and I'm not suggesting that people stop attending a church that is close to their hearts and is faithfully caring for their souls. However, I do want to point out the additional challenges that face commuter churches and the commitment it takes the members to overcome them. I also want to be clear that some of these challenges aren't unique to commuter churches. Any congregation that becomes an isolated gathering of people who are like an island in a sea of nonchurched neighbors faces these challenges.

The most significant challenge to identifying local people for outreach is that we don't know the local people. Whether we commute from another community where we do not know our neighbors or we live near our church but have isolated ourselves from the people around us, it's hard to reach out to people we don't know. Getting to know the people in the neighborhoods surrounding our congregation takes time and interaction. If our property is locked up and our members are elsewhere except on Sunday mornings, how are we going to get to know the local people? Also, what kind of message are we sending to our neighbors when our buildings sit vacant for most of the week and our members live far away? If we're going to be effective in reaching the local nonchurched people, we need to be local ourselves. That could mean members choosing to reside in the community or making the commute during the week, maybe even multiple times. In some way, we need to have an ongoing local presence to identify local people for outreach.

CHAPTER 9

Creating Effective Outreach Pathways

STEP 2: SELECT A PATHWAY CONDUIT

Using SNAIL helps us narrow our outreach focus to a specific type of nonchurched person in our community (i.e., our WHOM). With a clear idea of who we are focusing on for the outreach effort that we are planning, we can now start planning how we are going to engage the people we've identified. However, before we start putting together an Outreach Pathway, we need to identify the ministry or activity that is going to create opportunities for us to Create Connections, Nurture Relationships, and Make Disciples. These ministries and activities are called Pathway Conduits.

What Is a Pathway Conduit?

A Pathway Conduit is a ministry or activity that provides opportunities for us to Create Connections, Nurture Relationships, and Make Disciples through outreach activities that we plan and conduct alongside them. Think of a Pathway Conduit as something that your congregation is doing or could do that would be a gateway for nonchurched people to enter the Outreach Funnel.

When planning Pathway Conduits, it's important to keep in mind that the ministry or activity we identify takes place whether we conduct outreach or not. In other words, the Pathway Conduit is not an outreach activity itself but a ministry or activity that feeds people into the activities of the Outreach Pathway. Any ministry or activity that involves interaction with nonchurched people has the potential of serving as a Pathway Conduit. This means that the work of planning and conducting the ministry or activity that we identify as a Pathway Conduit is being done by the people responsible for that ministry or activity not by the people planning the Outreach Pathway. However, it also means that the people planning and executing Outreach Pathways need to coordinate their work with the people planning and conducting the ministry or activity that they identify as a Pathway Conduit.

What Makes for an Effective Pathway Conduit?

While any ministry or activity that provides interaction with non-churched people has the potential of being a Pathway Conduit, some activities make for better conduits than others. As a rule, we want to use activities that can feed people into the Create Connections and Nurture Relationships phases of the Outreach Process as Pathway Conduits. There's no need to use activities that feed people only into the Make Disciples phase, since no Outreach Pathway would be necessary in that case.

Some ministries or activities work well as conduits into the Create Connections phase of the Outreach Process. Others work better as conduits into the Nurture Relationships phase. For example, an annual event such as an Oktoberfest or Thanksgiving dinner could be an effective Pathway Conduit for feeding people into the Create Connections phase of the Outreach Process because it provides us with contact information. However, it wouldn't be a good conduit into the Nurture Relationships phase because it doesn't provide the ongoing engagement that is needed for building outreach relationships. On the other hand, an ongoing activity like a parenting class or support group could serve as a conduit into both the Create Connections and the Nurture Relationships

phases because it provides both a way to gather contact information and the ongoing interactions that build outreach relationships.

When considering Pathway Conduits, start with the things you
are already doing that provide or could provide you with interactions with the nonchurched people in your community. They may
be effective conduits as they currently are, or they may become
effective conduits with some minor adjustments. Using existing
activities as Pathway Conduits will help you get started with planning Outreach Pathways more quickly, break down barriers that
may exist in your congregation, and get more people on board
and involved in planning intentional, effective outreach.

ASSESSING A PATHWAY CONDUIT

Whether you are making use of an existing ministry or activity or
creating something new, the following six questions will help you
assess a potential Pathway Conduit. A ministry or activity for which
you can answer yes to all six of these questions has the greatest
potential for being an effective Pathway Conduit.

QUESTIONS FOR ASSESSING A PATHWAY CONDUIT
1. Does this ministry/activity address a need, concern, or interest of the nonchurched people in our community?
2. Is there room for us to do this ministry/activity in our community?
3. Is there a sufficient level of interest concerning this ministry/activity within our congregation?
4. Do we have or can we readily acquire the technical expertise required for this ministry/activity?
5. Are we able to fund this ministry/activity in a sustainable manner?
6. Do we have or can we create the capacity for this ministry/activity?

1. Does this ministry/activity address a need, concern, or interest of the nonchurched people in our community?

There are things we do in our congregation because they are of
interest and are appealing to us. That's okay. Not everything we

do has to be related to outreach. But if we are going to make use of something as a Pathway Conduit, it needs to be interesting and appealing to the nonchurched people in our community.

In a word, this approach to engaging and interacting with the nonchurched people in our community is called "attractional." The attractional approach for outreach recognizes that we need to offer something interesting and appealing to the nonchurched people around us if we are going to gain their attention and motivate them to participate in what we are offering. Unfortunately, the attractional approach to outreach has been abused by some churches and has ended up with a poor reputation. Those abuses are centered around changing our teachings or practices, especially worship practices, to be more appealing to people who don't belong to a church. The focus on getting people to come to worship services shows that these churches are not using attractional outreach properly. (Actually, their focus on getting people into worship services shows that they don't understand how to reach out to nonchurched people.)

Attractional outreach is properly used in the Create Connections and Nurture Relationships phases of the Outreach Process. It creates the opportunities for starting and continuing our outreach activities. Attractional outreach prepares people to join us in our faithful teachings and practices by using a Pathway Conduit to feed people into the Outreach Process, through which we can build outreach relationships. Through those outreach relationships, we can invite people into the Word-and-Sacrament ministry of our congregation through appropriate entry points, which may or may not be worship services.

If an activity doesn't address a need, concern, or interest of the nonchurched people in our community (i.e., if it is not attractional) we won't have any interactions with the nonchurched people around us. Without those interactions, we don't have ways to Create Connections, Nurture Relationships, and Make Disciples.

2. Is there room for us to do this ministry/activity in our community?

Sometimes we have a good idea for attracting and engaging nonchurched people in our community but there are already other people doing what we are considering. That may be okay, especially if the need or interest is greater than the current capacity of those doing the activity. But we may also find that there is not room for us to do this activity too.

If we're already doing something that engages the nonchurched people around us, we know that there is room for us to do it under the current circumstances. But if we are considering a new activity or ministry to use as a Pathway Conduit, we need to make sure that other organizations are not already doing something, or getting ready to do something, to meet the need or fulfill the interest. For example, if we recognize that there are unmet food needs for families in our neighborhood, we might consider opening a food pantry. As part of our consideration, we should check to see if other congregations or organizations in our community are already operating food pantries. If there are other food pantries in our community, we need to look into what days they are open and which groups of people they are serving. We should also check with the area's food bank to learn about pockets of unserved people, plans for future food pantries that we don't know about, and their opinion about us starting a food pantry.

Doing some research to determine if there is room in our community for something new may lead to some disappointment. We may discover that other congregations, nonprofit organizations, or governmental agencies have already addressed an interest or need of the people we are hoping to reach out to. But it's better to experience that disappointment when investigating than to put a lot of time, money, and energy into something that won't attract or engage nonchurched people because it is already being done by others in our community.

3. Is there a sufficient level of interest concerning this ministry/activity within our congregation?

We may come up with a ministry or activity that captures the interest of the nonchurched people in our community and determine that no other organization is providing what we're considering, but we also need to make sure that there is enough interest in our congregation to plan, start, and continue the activity. This is not only true about the things that we're considering doing but is also true about things we are already doing, to make sure there is enough interest and support to keep it going.

Gauging the level of interest in the congregation is more art than science. You can get a good sense of how much support a ministry or activity has in the congregation by the conversations people are having about it. If there is a sense of excitement about the activity, there is probably a decent amount of support for it. Don't assume that there is adequate support for the activity just because it passed a vote by the congregation. I've been to many voters' meetings during which a motion was passed overwhelmingly, but very few people in the congregation had much interest in getting involved in it or supporting it. If something passed at the last voters' meeting but no one is expressing any further interest in it, the activity is likely to lack the support that it needs. Of course, if there is significant opposition to a ministry or activity—even if approved by a vote by a board or the congregation—it is a poor choice for a Pathway Conduit.

Another thing to consider about how much support an activity actually has is whether there are enough people in the congregation who are committed to doing the work required to plan and conduct the activity. Remember, the people planning the Outreach Pathway will not be planning and conducting the activity under consideration as a Pathway Conduit. There needs to be other interested and committed members of the congregation to ensure that the activity serving as a Pathway Conduit is taking place as planned.

4. **Do we have or can we readily acquire the technical expertise required for this ministry/activity?**

Your congregation is filled with talented people who possess abundant gifts by God's grace. But that doesn't mean that you can do anything that you come up with as an idea for a Pathway Conduit. You may not have the expertise, experience, or qualifications for a particular activity. In some cases, you may find that there are resources and materials available for training to do the activity. In other cases, the requirements may currently be outside of the reach of your congregation, and you'll need to find a different activity to use as a Pathway Conduit.

Suppose that your congregation decides that starting an after-school tutoring program would provide you with a good Pathway Conduit. There's a lot of interest and support for this activity in the congregation. You check into the requirements and find that you meet the rules and regulations of your state and local government. You've been blessed with many members who have retired from their occupations and want to help plan and conduct the tutoring program, including some who were teachers. In this case, you have the technical expertise that is needed to undertake the activity.

Now suppose that your congregation decides that a preschool would be a good Pathway Conduit. You know that there are state and local regulations that you must meet, but you aren't familiar with them. You've been told that you need to be licensed and that you'll need a qualified director. You have members who are willing to help with the preschool, but none of them have any experience, let alone the required certifications. It's clear that you don't have the technical expertise needed to plan, launch, and operate a preschool. However, it may still be a viable candidate for serving as a Pathway Conduit if you can acquire the technical expertise that you need. Hiring a qualified preschool director to manage the planning and startup of the preschool could help your congregation achieve the goal of operating a preschool that could also function as a Pathway Conduit.

5. Are we able to fund this ministry/activity in a sustainable manner?

Sometimes a great idea for a Pathway Conduit is not a practical idea from a financial point of view. Every congregation has to manage limited financial resources in ways that meet all the needs of the congregation. An activity may have tremendous potential as a Pathway Conduit, but if we can't fund it on an ongoing basis, it isn't going to be an effective Pathway Conduit for us. Please note the word *ongoing* when it comes to funding the activity. Raising the funds to get an activity up and running isn't enough. We also need to have a source of funding the activity for the foreseeable future.

When planning the funding to sustain an activity that is serving as a Pathway Conduit, don't fall into the trap of thinking that it will somehow provide its own funding by bringing new people into the congregation or generating revenue for the congregation. I can speak to this from painful experience. As a church planter, I embraced a model of church planting through early childhood ministry. I could see the outreach potential of this model. Not only that, but I was also enticed by the promise that it would not only be self-funding but would also generate excess revenue that could be used to fund the church plant. On paper, it looked like the perfect way to plant a congregation. As far as outreach goes, it was very successful. We reached many nonchurched people in our community, and I had the privilege of baptizing many children and several families. Financially it was a disaster. There was no plan for funding the early childhood ministry other than the revenue it generated—which never came close to what had been projected. In time, the financial burden overwhelmed the early childhood ministry and the congregation.

6. **Do we have or can we create the capacity for this ministry/activity?**

When it comes to capacity, each ministry or activity has its own requirements. Some activities require a lot of space or specialized facilities. Others call for specific equipment or technology. You may have to comply with governmental regulations or your insurance provider's requirements for some activities. Whatever the capacity requirements are for an activity or ministry that you are considering as a Pathway Conduit, make sure that your congregation has the capacity for it or can create the capacity required.

When considering capacity, don't forget to take the capacity of the people in your congregation into consideration. Even with adequate support, funding, technical expertise, and other elements of capacity, an activity that requires people to do more than they are already doing may prove to be too much. Making use of existing ministries and activities as Pathway Conduits is one way to ensure that you have the capacity to do something. Another way is to increase your congregation's capacity by encouraging people who are not currently involved in a ministry or activity to take a role in the new ministry or activity that you've identified as a Pathway Conduit. Either way, take into consideration that there are limits to what people are able and willing to do when assessing your congregation's capacity for planning and conducting an activity that you'd like to use as a Pathway Conduit.

CHAPTER 10

Creating Effective Outreach Pathways

STEP 3: IDENTIFY AND EVALUATE PATHWAY ACTIVITIES

> The crucible is for silver, and the furnace is for gold, and the **LORD tests hearts.**   PROVERBS 17:3

Once you've identified the people you are seeking to engage through your outreach efforts (i.e., your WHOM) and have selected a ministry or activity as a Pathway Conduit, you're ready to start putting the Outreach Pathway together. The building blocks of the Outreach Pathway are called Pathway Activities.

Pathway Activities are new or existing ministries and activities that you can use to Create Connections, Nurture Relationships, and Make Disciples. It's likely that your congregation is already doing things that will work well as Pathway Activities or that will work well with only a few minor changes. It's also likely that you'll need to add some new activities or ministries to build effective Outreach Pathways for many of the WHOMs you would like to reach out to.

Some ministries or activities are most effective as Create Connections activities. Others are most effective as Nurture Relationships or Make Disciples activities. As part of building the Outreach Pathway for a WHOM, we need to identify which ministries might work best in each phase of the Outreach Process and then evaluate them for the pathway that we are creating for the specific type of person we've identified for this outreach effort (i.e., our WHOM).

It might seem overwhelming to identify and evaluate Pathway Activities to build multiple Outreach Pathways for different kinds of nonchurched people, but keep in mind that an activity can be used on multiple pathways. For example, you may identify a parenting class as Outreach Activity in the Nurture Relationships phase of an Outreach Pathway for married men with young children. That same parenting class could also be an Outreach Activity for married women with young children or for single mothers. However, it wouldn't be a good Outreach Activity for newly retired couples.

Using an activity in a pathway depends on the WHOM of that pathway. When we evaluate a ministry or activity to determine if it could be an Outreach Activity for the Outreach Pathway we are developing, we want to assess it according to that pathway's WHOM.

Evaluating Pathway Activities

The following seven questions will help you assess a ministry or activity to determine if it should be included in the Outreach Pathway you are developing for a particular WHOM. Use these questions each time you create a unique pathway, keeping in mind that how you answer the questions for an activity depends as much on the WHOM of the pathway as on the activity itself. You will probably discover that a Pathway Activity that doesn't work well for one WHOM may be great for a different WHOM.

QUESTIONS FOR EVALUATING PATHWAY ACTIVITIES		
Question	**Phase(s) of Outreach Process**	**Focus/Purpose**
1. What about this activity would WHOM find interesting or appealing?	All	Looking at outreach activities from the WHOM's perspective
2. How does this activity provide a way for our congregation to continue contact with WHOM?	Create Connections	Ensuring we have a means of continuing contact with WHOM
3. Why would WHOM be willing to participate in this activity?	All, especially Nurture Relationships	Considering obstacles that may keep an interested WHOM from participating
4. How does this activity help our members engage WHOM on an ongoing basis?	Nurture Relationships	Bringing members and our WHOM together repeatedly over time
5. How have we equipped our members for using this activity to nurture relationships with WHOM?	Nurture Relationships	Identifying ways to equip members for nurturing outreach relationships
6. To which entry points into the Word-and-Sacrament ministry of our congregation does this activity guide WHOM?	Make Disciples	Identifying entry points into Word-and-Sacrament ministry
7. Why would WHOM be interested in participating in the Word-and-Sacrament ministry of our congregation through this activity?	Make Disciples	Considering obstacles that may keep an interested WHOM from participating

1. **What about this activity would WHOM find interesting or appealing?**

This question applies to ministries and activities for all phases of the Outreach Process. It speaks to the I of SNAIL. When considering this question, put yourself in the place of the WHOM. Why would this person be interested in this activity? What need does it address? How will the person perceive the activity as we are presenting it? We've already discussed the importance of considering the perspective of nonchurched people when planning outreach efforts. Asking this question for each activity being considered will help us make sure that the activity is of interest and is appealing to the WHOM of the pathway. It reinforces that we aren't simply identifying activities that are generally appealing to nonchurched people but that we are identifying activities that are specifically of interest to the type of people we are seeking to engage through this particular pathway.

2. **How does this activity provide a way for our congregation to continue contact with WHOM?**

This question is focused on Create Connections activities. Working through the answers to this question will help ensure that we don't miss opportunities to continue our outreach efforts with the nonchurched people we engage through an event or activity that provides a point of connection between them and our congregation. We may find that there is already something that is part of this activity that enables us to gather the information we need to continue contact (e.g., enrolling in a class). We may also find that we need to add something to an activity in order to collect the desired information (e.g., adding a registration for a door prize at a social event).

3. **Why would WHOM be willing to participate in this activity?**

This question can be used for activities in all phases of the Outreach Process, but it is especially important for the Nurture Relationships phase. It is related to the question about the activity being of interest or appealing to the WHOM of the pathway, but it goes further than interest to consider action. We should be mindful of the things that might keep a person from participating in an activity even when she finds it appealing and interesting. Anything from not having time in her schedule to being uncomfortable attending a church-sponsored activity can keep a person from participating in the activity we are planning. Wrestling with this question will help us identify potential obstacles and prompt us to plan ways to overcome them.

4. **How does this activity help our members engage WHOM on an ongoing basis?**

This question is focused on activities in the Nurture Relationships phase of the Outreach Process. It addresses two important aspects of developing and strengthening outreach relationships. First, it asks us to consider how this activity will bring together the nonchurched people and members of our congregation. We can't nurture relationships with nonchurched people if we aren't interacting with them. Second, this question underscores that we need to provide ways for the WHOM and our members to have ongoing interactions over time. In other words, we need to avoid "one and done" activities.

5. **How have we equipped our members for using this activity to nurture relationships with WHOM?**

This question also focuses on Nurture Relationships activities. It raises the issue of equipping our members for starting and developing outreach relationships. Not only do we want to train and support members of our congregation with relationship-building skills in general, but we also want to consider what specific relationship-building skills would be most appropriate for this particular outreach activity. For example, the relationship-building skills that would be most effective for outreach relationships between couples attending a marriage enrichment class are different from the skills that would be effective for building an outreach relationship between a tutor and a student in an after-school tutoring program.

6. **To which entry points into the Word-and-Sacrament ministry of our congregation does this activity guide WHOM?**

This question addresses activities that bridge the Nurture Relationships and Make Disciples phases of the Outreach Process. It is an important question to consider for outreach activities in the later stages of relationship building—when we've moved from "few to many" and have developed mutual trust and respect with our WHOM. Through the outreach relationships that we have developed with nonchurched people, we should have a good sense of which entry points into our Word-and-Sacrament ministry will be of interest and appealing to our WHOM. Through those relationships, we'll also have insight into which entry points are most appropriate.

7. **Why would WHOM be interested in participating in the Word-and-Sacrament ministry of our congregation through this activity?**

This final question for evaluating Pathway Activities specifically applies to those activities that are part of our congregation's Word-and-Sacrament ministry. We especially want to consider the activities that serve as entry points into our Word-and-Sacrament ministry when considering an activity that may be included in an Outreach Pathway. While we may think that we've identified ways for nonchurched people to join us in our Word-and-Sacrament ministry that are inviting and nonthreatening, this question challenges us to look at those activities from our WHOM's perspective.

Using the Outreach Funnel to Organize Pathway Activities

The Outreach Funnel is a useful tool for capturing and organizing the Pathway Activities that we've evaluated for a particular WHOM.

Each of the activities that we've determined to be useful for engaging nonchurched people can be recorded in the appropriate section of the Outreach Funnel for reference. Then, as we build pathways for a particular WHOM, we can refer to the Outreach Funnel to use the activities that we've already evaluated. This approach saves a lot of time and effort by capturing the evaluation of the Pathway Activities. It uses the Outreach Funnel to build a library of the ministries and activities that we can use for Outreach Pathways. We can tap into that library when building an Outreach Pathway for a WHOM.

I find that using a poster with a diagram of the Outreach Funnel and sticky notes with the Pathway Activities written on them (one per sticky note) is a simple and straightforward way of using the Outreach Funnel as a catalog of Pathway Activities for the Outreach Pathways we're about to create for our WHOM. Putting a diagram of the Outreach Funnel on a whiteboard and then using sticky notes to arrange the Pathway Activities also works well. You may have a different method of cataloging the Pathway Activities. Use what works best for you and your congregation. Whatever method you use to manage the results of evaluating Pathway Activities, make sure that you keep things focused on the WHOM you're about to create Outreach Pathways for.

CHAPTER 11

Creating Effective Outreach Pathways

STEP 4: ARRANGE AND CAPTURE OUTREACH PATHWAYS

> So Philip ran to [the eunuch] and heard him reading Isaiah the prophet and asked, "Do you understand what you are reading?" And he said, "How can I, unless someone guides me?" And he invited Philip to come up and sit with him.
>
> ACTS 8:30–31

When Philip approached the Ethiopian eunuch, he found the man reading the prophet Isaiah. There's no explanation for why the man was reading God's Word or how he obtained a copy of Isaiah, which was unusual at that time. All we know is that he had an interest in God's Word and that he needed someone to guide him in understanding it. When we engage the nonchurched people in our community, we can be sure of two things: they need the Word of God, and they need someone to guide them. As Philip was called to guide the Ethiopian eunuch in understanding God's Word and to prepare him to receive the gift of Holy Baptism, we are called to guide people into God's Means of Grace. Philip used a chariot ride to guide the eunuch. We can use Outreach Pathways.

To get a better idea of what goes into capturing an Outreach Pathway, we're going to look at two examples. Before we examine these examples, let's review and elaborate on the things we need to keep in mind when we are creating pathways.

An Effective Pathway Focuses on a Single and Specific WHOM

As guides, Outreach Pathways are most helpful when they are focused and simple. Keeping a pathway focused involves centering it on a single and specific type of person (i.e., our WHOM). The acronym SNAIL (Specific, Nonchurched, Accessible, Interested, and Local) helps us focus our pathway. Keeping our pathways simple can be challenging because we tend to try to do too much in a single pathway. It's much better to create multiple pathways for a single WHOM than to put together some master pathway that considers every possibility for that WHOM. I've seen Outreach Pathways with lines going multiple directions, looping back, and crisscrossing each other. They looked like someone had dropped a potful of cooked spaghetti. They were not useful guides. Creating useful guides calls for a different approach.

Instead of attempting to create one comprehensive Outreach Pathway for a WHOM, we should plan multiple Outreach Pathways for each WHOM. While it sounds like more work to create multiple simpler pathways instead of a single comprehensive pathway, in the long run it ends up being less work—and much less work to maintain them. More important, multiple simpler pathways are more effective guides and more likely to be used than confusing "spaghetti charts."

An Effective Pathway Identifies Outreach Efforts but Does Not Plan Ministries or Activities

Even the simplest Outreach Pathway contains multiple ministries and activities. If the pathway included all the work to plan and conduct the ministries and activities, it would be complicated and overwhelming. Rather than trying to plan or manage the ministries and activities, a pathway simply identifies the ministries and activities that will be used to help us help nonchurched people progress through the Outreach Process. This means that we have to count on other people in the congregation to plan and conduct the activities that we identify as Pathway Conduits or include in the Outreach Pathway.

It's tempting to include the planning or management of the activities that we identify for our outreach efforts in the Outreach Pathway. It's especially tempting to do so when we identify a new ministry or activity for outreach or when we have a special interest in an activity. But including that kind of detail in an Outreach Pathway will make the pathway far too complicated to be useful as a guide for outreach.

I was once facilitating an outreach workshop for a small congregation that didn't have a youth group. One of the participants was passionate about starting a youth group for the high school students in their congregation. She decided that the outreach workshop was a good opportunity to plan how to start the youth group. I wasn't able to convince her to stop at identifying the activities that they needed to reach nonchurched high school youth in their community and to do the planning for the youth group separately from the planning of the Outreach Pathway. The resulting pathway was a reasonably good plan for starting a high school youth group but it had almost nothing to do with outreach.

Stopping at identifying ministries and activities (either new or existing) when planning a pathway doesn't mean that we can ignore the work that needs to be done to plan and conduct them. Somebody needs to plan and manage the activities that make up the pathway. That's why the Outreach Pathway is divided into swim lanes that are each assigned to an individual who is responsible for making sure that the activities in her lane are being planned and conducted.

An Effective Pathway Demonstrates Who Ensures What at Each Stage of the Pathway

The swim lanes of the Outreach Pathway are important for making sure that someone in the congregation is responsible for ensuring that the activities in the pathway are being conducted. This is different than making someone responsible for planning and executing the activities. The responsibility of the person assigned to a swim lane is to ensure that the appropriate board, committee, team, or individual is aware of the plan to use the activity for outreach, to coordinate any logistics to use the activity for outreach, and to communicate information about the activity that may affect the Outreach Pathway.

The swim lanes in an Outreach Pathway are not used to show who *does* what but are used to show who *ensures* what. There is a significant difference between these two responsibilities. "Who does what" demonstrates who is responsible for planning and conducting a ministry or activity—something we do not want included in an Outreach Pathway. "Who ensures what" demonstrates who is going to ensure that the ministry or activity will be available for use as an Outreach Activity as planned. The role of the person assigned to an Outreach Pathway swim lane is to coordinate and communicate, not to plan and execute.

It's important to identify an individual for each swim lane rather than a board, committee, or team. By naming one and only one person at the top of a swim lane, there is a clear assignment of responsibility for ensuring that the activities in that swim lane will be available for outreach. If multiple people are assigned to a swim lane (e.g., a board or committee), it become less clear as to who is responsible for ensuring the availability of the activities in that swim lane. If a board, committee, or team ends up with the responsibility for a swim lane, ask them to designate one person as the point of contact for the group and use that person's name for the Outreach Pathway.

Another thing to avoid when putting together a pathway is combining swim lanes to save on space. It's not unusual for a swim lane to have only one activity. It's tempting to combine a couple of sparsely populated swim lanes to create some room on the pathway for the other swim lanes. While this may help balance out the pathway diagram, combining swim lanes creates confusion about who is responsible for the swim lane. It is better to add more swim lanes to a pathway than to combine them to consolidate space. By adding swim lanes, you will be able to maintain the assignment of one responsible person to the lane.

If you don't have a person to assign to a swim lane, leave it blank. A blank entry at the top of a swim lane is a visual reminder that action is needed to resolve the assignment of the swim lane. It's easy to overlook that action item if the swim lane has been filled in with a board, committee, or team name as a placeholder. Leaving the swim lane entry blank will make it stand out as a potential obstacle or gap.

An Effective Pathway Answers "What's Next?"

When planning an Outreach Pathway, don't lose sight of the purpose of the pathway. We're creating the pathway as a plan to help us help nonchurched people move through the Outreach Process. The pathway is our plan for intentional outreach. It captures what we intend to do to help people move from a connection into relationships and from relationships into our Word-and-Sacrament ministry. It reflects movement.

To capture the movement of an Outreach Pathway, we want to keep asking ourselves the question "What's next?" as we add Pathway Activities to the pathway. Starting with the activity or event that creates the connection with our WHOM, we ask ourselves "What's next?" to figure out what activity (or activities) can be used to start outreach relationships. The first relationship-building activities should involve a small number of members of the congregation to support the few-to-many approach to building outreach relationships. From those initial relationship-building activities, we want to ask ourselves "What's next?" to include activities in the pathway that will expand and strengthen the outreach relationships. Asking and answering "What's next?" will also guide us in using activities as entry points into the Word-and-Sacrament ministry of our congregation.

Use lines to map out the flow of the Outreach Pathway. (If possible, use lines with arrows on the right end). Lines from one Outreach Activity to another make clear the answer to "What's next?" It's common to have more than one line going from or coming into an Outreach Activity, but don't get carried away. The Outreach Pathway is meant to be a simple and straightforward plan, not a diagram that exhausts every possibility. Keep the lines simple.

When mapping out an Outreach Pathway, make sure that the movement is always from left to right (i.e., from Create Connections to Make Disciples). Because pathways answer the question "What's next?" the flow of the pathway never goes backwards (i.e., from right to left). If necessary, you can rearrange the swim lanes to maintain the proper flow of a pathway—one that captures the logical progression through the Outreach Process from one Outreach Activity to the next. Don't forget to consider the few-to-many orientation of the Nurture Relationships phase when mapping out the pathway.

Adding the lines is the final step in diagraming an Outreach Pathway. To complete the pathway, review the diagram to ensure that there are no obstacles or gaps in the pathway. Gaps are easy to find. They are identified by broken pathway flows. Those breaks occur whenever an Outreach Activity does not have a line coming into or going out of it. Obstacles are harder to identify because they are more about logic than mechanics. One example of an obstacle is a line that jumps over the Nurture Relationships section of the Outreach Pathway. Another example is a series of "one and done" events in place of an activity that provides ongoing interaction for building outreach relationships.

Example Pathways

Describing Outreach Pathways and their characteristics may make them seem complicated or confusing. But effective pathways are actually simple and straightforward. After you've put together a few pathways, you'll see that there isn't anything complicated about them. But before you put some together, let's work through a couple of hypothetical examples. These examples involve two similar Lutheran congregations. They both have day schools and are working to improve their outreach to the nonchurched families that have children enrolled in their schools.

We'll use the four steps for creating Outreach Pathways to evaluate the Outreach Pathways that the two congregations created.

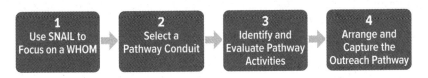

OUTREACH PATHWAYS EXAMPLE 1:
GRACE LUTHERAN CHURCH AND SCHOOL (GLCS)

GLCS Background

Grace Lutheran Church and School (GLCS) has a K–8 school with ninety students. There was little interaction between the congregation members and the school during the fifteen-year tenure of the previous pastor. Pastor Kevin Warner has served the congregation for about two years. He is more supportive of the school but not greatly involved.

To strengthen the bond between the congregation and the school, Pastor Warner convinced the school board to require one of the school choirs to sing once a month in the Divine Service as outreach to the nonchurched families. Some of the parents of the nonchurched students asked for their children to be excused because it interfered with sports and other activities. Parents who belonged to other churches also requested to have their children excused because it conflicted with their participation in their own churches. But participation was made part of the students' grades for the music class. Most parents complied, though some were rather reluctant—and irritated.

Several congregational members, including two elders, complained to Pastor Warner about the behavior of the nonchurched families during the worship service. Several of the parents videorecorded their children singing, cheered when the children were finished, and left the service as soon as the choir had sung. The members felt that the parents were being rude and disrespectful. Rather than strengthening the bond between the congregation and the school, the required singing was creating a lot of tension between Pastor Warner, the teachers, the congregational members, and the parents. Nonetheless, Pastor Warner insisted that they continue to require the singing as outreach.

After meeting with the elders and then the school staff to discuss the complaints about nonchurched families disrupting the worship service, Pastor Warner decided to drop the requirement for the choirs to sing on Sundays. The choirs would still sing, but participation would be voluntary. With a few exceptions, the nonchurched families stopped attending the worship services in which the choirs were singing.

Realizing that they needed a different approach for outreach to the nonchurched families with children enrolled in their school, Pastor Warner met with the evangelism committee to plan some activities. After discussing how to improve the congregation's outreach through their school ministry, the evangelism committee decided to put together an Outreach Pathway for reaching out to the nonchurched school families and present it to the church council for approval and support. They identified ten activities (see the table) to include in the Outreach Pathway for their nonchurched school families.

ACTIVITY	DESCRIPTION
Family Fun Night	A monthly night for families to come to the church to play games, have seasonal parties, enjoy movie nights, and more.
Moms' Night Out/ Date Night	A once-a-month weekday evening on which the congregation provides free childcare for nonchurched families to allow the parents to have a night off
Parenting Class	A class for improving parenting skills
Monthly Dinner	A family dinner provided by the congregation
Touch-a-Truck Event	A fun day of games, food, and different kinds of vehicles for kids to explore (e.g., police car, fire truck, dump truck)
Bible 101	A four-week study that provides an introduction to the Bible and the basic teachings of the Christian Faith
Toddler Play Date	Twice-a-month time for moms (or dads) and their toddlers to enjoy some play time together at the church
Marriage Enrichment Weekends	A marriage workshop led by the pastor during a weekend retreat
Book Club	A monthly informal gathering during school hours to discuss a book that has some kind of Christian teachings or content
Emergency Response Training	A two-weekend training session to equip people with basic emergency response skills (e.g., first aid, CPR)

Using these ideas for Pathway Activities and some existing ministries and activities, the committee put together the following Outreach Pathway.

GLCS's Outreach Pathway

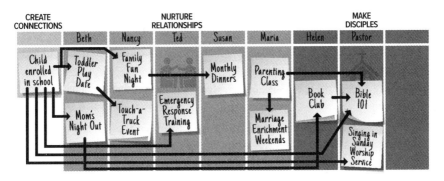

Evaluating GLCS's Outreach Pathway

1. **Use SNAIL to Focus on a WHOM**—The planners started with the broad category of "Parents of Nonchurched Students" but didn't do anything to focus on a specific type of person for this outreach effort. Without a focus on a specific WHOM, the Pathway Activities that they identified covered a wide range of interests. On the plus side, they did identify a group of nonchurched people who are local and who are accessible to the congregation.

2. **Select a Pathway Conduit**—Given the focus of GLCS's outreach discussion, the school ministry was chosen as the Pathway Conduit before they started planning the Outreach Pathway. Choosing a Pathway Conduit can be a good starting point for planning an Outreach Pathway when looking at how to make use of existing ministries or activities for outreach. The key to doing this effectively is to make sure that you use SNAIL to focus on a WHOM before identifying Pathway Activities.

3. **Identify and Evaluate Pathway Activities**—Unfortunately, GLCS's planners did not use SNAIL to focus on a WHOM before they started identifying activities to build a pathway. While many of the ministries and activities they identified are effective for outreach, the lack of a specific WHOM resulted in a variety of unrelated and unfocused activities. For example, a "Moms' Night Out" might be of interest to nonchurched women with children in the school, but it wouldn't appeal to men. The "Touch-a-Truck" event might draw families with young children but wouldn't be of much interest to families with older children. GLCS's diverse list of Pathway Activities shows the importance of considering your WHOM when identifying ministries and activities that can be used for outreach.

4. **Arrange and Capture the Outreach Pathway**—The resulting pathway has several problems. Before we look at the problems, let's highlight a couple of the things that GLCS did right. They clearly identified an event that started the Outreach Pathway with "Child enrolled in school," and they used that as the starting point for most of the activities in the pathway. They also did a good job in defining the swim lanes by naming one specific

person for each lane and keeping activities within a single lane. Despite the busyness of the pathway, they consistently maintained a left-to-right flow.

The problems with their pathway stem from failing to identify a specific WHOM. As a result, we see several activities that aren't clearly related to one another. The multiple arrow lines coming out of the Create Connections event provides a visual clue that the activities are unrelated. When the Pathway Activities are focused on a specific WHOM, the relationship between the activities will result in fewer lines from the Create Connections event because they flow from one to another.

The lines in this Outreach Pathway also highlight that there are several obstacles and gaps built into the pathway. Gaps are evident where nothing follows an activity in the pathway. Notice that there are no lines going from Touch-a-Truck Event, Emergency Response Training, Monthly Dinners, and Marriage Enrichment Weekends. Gaps are also visually demonstrated by activities with no lines feeding into them. In this pathway, there are no activities leading people into the Parenting Class activity. Obstacles are visible where lines skip over the Nurture Relationships section of the pathway, which is the case for Singing in Sunday Worship Service and one of the lines for Bible 101. While it's possible that people will accept an invitation that will move them directly from the connection point into our Word-and-Sacrament ministry—praise God when they do!—it isn't something that we should count on. Our outreach plan should show how we intend to help them move from connection into relationship building and then into our Word-and-Sacrament ministry.

The complexity of this Outreach Pathway makes it hard to follow. It's unlikely to be used as it is. To make it useful, it should be broken down into multiple simpler pathways that are focused on specific WHOMs.

OUTREACH PATHWAYS EXAMPLE 2:
EMMANUEL LUTHERAN CHURCH AND SCHOOL (ELCS)

ELCS Background

Emmanuel Lutheran Church and School (ELCS) is a PreK–8 school with 120 students. The pastor, Rev. Dr. Michael Grant, and the congregation are very supportive of the school. Pastor Grant teaches the seventh- and eighth-grade religion classes and conducts a weekly chapel service that is attended by all students. He also eats lunch with the students (usually the seventh and eighth graders) at least twice a week.

About twelve congregational members without children in the school volunteer for school activities, including being library readers, serving as adoptive grandparents for students without local grandparents, coaching sports teams, and tutoring children in the after-school care program. They recently started a tutoring program for students who don't use the after-school program. There are wonderful relationships between the volunteers and the nonchurched students, but those relationships tend to end when the students leave Emmanuel's school.

Interaction with the parents of nonchurched students is limited. Pastor Grant offers a special adult instruction class for nonchurched school parents. Up to now it has been a voluntary class with few participants. The pastor was planning on making it mandatory for all parents who are not members of Emmanuel to increase his interaction with them. However, after meeting with the school's principal, Mr. Tom Franklin, he is reconsidering that plan. The principal pointed out that making the class mandatory may alienate some parents and intimidate others. He also challenged Pastor Grant by asking him, "What is it that you're actually trying to accomplish with this class?"

After his meeting with Mr. Franklin, Pastor Grant got together with a couple of the outreach-minded elders and the chairman (and only member) of the Evangelism Committee, Bob Richards. Through their discussions, they decided to start planning outreach efforts for specific types of people who make up the nonchurched families with children enrolled in their school.

Pastor Grant pointed out that the children in the school are already hearing God's Word through their religion classes and weekly chapel. He suggested that they focus on engaging the parents of the nonchurched students. He also shared his insight from his conversation with Mr. Franklin that the nonchurched parents are not all alike. He asked the group which parents they thought they should focus on first.

Mike Wagner, an elder and a financial planner, pointed out that there were many school families who were struggling to make tuition payments. He suggested that they focus on couples who would be interested in improving their family finances. After discussing how they might engage such couples, the team came up with the following ideas for Pathway Activities:

ACTIVITY	DESCRIPTION
Family Finances Class	A financial management class that teaches budgeting and basic financial planning (though not biblical stewardship)
Money in the Bible	A Bible study on biblical stewardship
Meal Prep	Using the church kitchen to learn recipes and prepare low-cost meals
Family Fun Night	A monthly no-cost family activity night
Basic Car Care and Repair	A basic car-care cooperative where people can learn general maintenance and simple repairs
Book Club for Moms	A book club for moms with free childcare and refreshments that meets in the evenings to accommodate working moms
Sewing and Quilting Class	A sewing and quilting class to teach people how to make and mend clothing, quilts, and other household items
Learn a DIY Skill Workshop	A monthly do-it-yourself workshop through which some of the members of the congregation who are active or retired from a trade can teach basic skills

After looking over their ideas, the team decided to refine their focus for their first Outreach Pathway. They then planned an

Outreach Pathway for nonchurched parents of children enrolled in the school who are interested in improving their family finances.

ELCS's Outreach Pathway

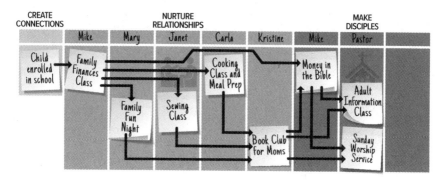

Evaluating ELCS's Outreach Pathway

1. **Use SNAIL to Focus on a WHOM**—Notice how the planners at ELCS started with a WHOM and then realized it wasn't specific enough. This was a helpful realization that enabled them to narrow the focus of the Outreach Pathway to a more specific type of nonchurched person. The resulting WHOM (nonchurched school parents who want to improve their family finances) provides the focus needed to create a simple and straightforward pathway. As this example shows, it's a good practice to review your WHOM as you build an Outreach Pathway and make any necessary adjustments using SNAIL as a guide.

2. **Select a Pathway Conduit**—The school ministry was chosen as the Pathway Conduit before the ELCS planners started planning the Outreach Pathway. It can be helpful to have a Pathway Conduit assigned on the front end of planning a pathway because it narrows the scope of the nonchurched people in the community to those who are engaged in or may be engaged in the ministry or activity selected as the conduit.

3. **Identify and Evaluate Pathway Activities**—The team planning this Outreach Pathway did a good job identifying ministries and activities that would be of interest and appealing to the WHOM that they initially selected (nonchurched school parents who

would be interested in improving their family finances). They also did a good job filtering the activities that they identified to fit the new, more specific WHOM. By keeping their WHOM in mind, they were able to identify Pathway Activities that are useful for engaging the nonchurched people they are focusing on.

4. **Arrange and Capture the Outreach Pathway**—ELCS's pathway is focused and simple. It is easy to follow, starting with Family Finances Class, which is the one activity after the Create Connections event. Following the lines from Family Finances Class, the pathway clearly shows four activities to which the WHOMs attending the class can be invited. The left-to-right flow of the pathway is maintained, but the few-to-many outreach relationships pattern isn't as strong as it could be. The one possible gap is that the Adult Information Class doesn't lead into Sunday Morning Worship (or vice versa).

One thing that is especially interesting about this pathway is that Mike shows up in two different swim lanes. This was done to maintain the left-to-right flow of the pathway and to show that Mike was responsible for Pathway Activities in both the Nurture Relationships and the Make Disciples phases of the Outreach Process. It's a good idea to assign a person to more than one swim lane to keep the flow of the pathway moving from left to right. When you do, make sure that the person assigned to multiple swim lanes is aware of all assignments.

If you look over the list of activities that ELCS put together to build a pathway, you'll notice that a couple of those activities were not included on the pathway they created. Excluding those activities was a good way to keep this pathway focused and simple. The activities that were not used on this pathway can be used for creating an additional pathway for this WHOM or for another WHOM. This pathway is a good example of making sure that you're not trying to do too much in a single pathway. Keeping a pathway simple makes it easy to follow and easy to maintain. As a rule, it's better to create additional pathways for a WHOM than to add more activities and lines to one like this example.

CHAPTER 12

BUILDING YOUR OUTREACH PATHWAYS

Our discussion about the Outreach Process and its supporting tools, the information about outreach that we've discussed, and the examples from Grace Lutheran Church and School and Emmanuel Lutheran Church and School have given you the information and resources that you need to create Outreach Pathways. You are well-versed and well-equipped to build pathways for your outreach efforts. Now let's put all this into practice by creating Outreach Pathways for your congregation.

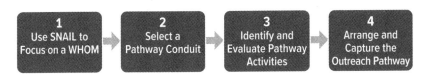

The four steps for creating Outreach Pathways are your guide for putting together effective pathways. Using these steps each time you develop new pathways will help you stay focused and will make sure that all the people involved in creating the pathways are working together. It's especially important to follow the four steps when you are working with people who are new to planning outreach efforts using this approach.

Step 1. Use SNAIL to Focus on a WHOM

Identifying a single and specific type of nonchurched person for an Outreach Pathway is a critical step in creating effective pathways. Before you create your first Outreach Pathway, consider putting together a diagram of the nonchurched people in your community. Use this diagram as a master list of the nonchurched people who live near your congregation. Set it up like a hierarchical organization chart so people can readily see how to identify a specific WHOM. Creating and maintaining a chart like this will provide you with a quick reference tool that will save you from having to start from scratch each time you begin the process of creating an Outreach Pathway. The actual divisions of nonchurched people in your chart will depend on the makeup of your community. The following chart is the beginning of a comprehensive listing of the nonchurched people in a typical community.

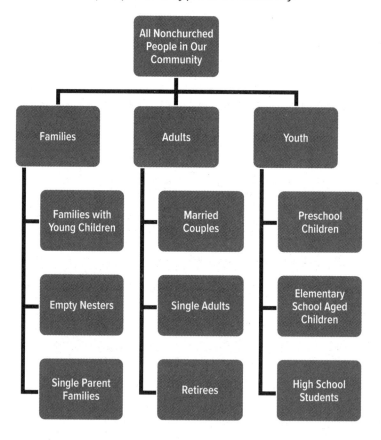

However you decide to go about doing it, make sure that you identify a WHOM for your Outreach Pathway that addresses each aspect of SNAIL. To do that, you may find it helpful to use a poster or whiteboard to record how the WHOM being considered meets the criteria of SNAIL. Go through each of the elements of SNAIL to identify a single and specific type of nonchurched person as the subject of your pathway.

WHOM – <u>W</u>ho <u>H</u>as <u>O</u>ur <u>M</u>ission focus	
Specific	
Nonchurched	
Accessible	
Interested	
Local	

Sample Poster for Identifying a WHOM Using SNAIL as a Guide

Step 2. Select a Pathway Conduit

Once you have your WHOM identified, choose a ministry or activity to use as a Pathway Conduit. You may have selected a Pathway Conduit before you identified your WHOM (as in our examples above). That's fine as long as you have clearly identified your WHOM before evaluating the Pathway Conduit. Once you have identified your WHOM and selected a ministry or activity for a Pathway Conduit, use the six questions for assessing a Pathway Conduit to determine if this activity has the potential to be an effective Pathway Conduit. As you consider these questions, make sure that you keep your WHOM in mind.

QUESTIONS FOR ASSESSING A PATHWAY CONDUIT
1. Does this ministry/activity address a need, concern, or interest of the nonchurched people in our community?
2. Is there room for us to do this ministry/activity in our community?
3. Is there a sufficient level of interest concerning this ministry/activity within our congregation?
4. Do we have or can we readily acquire the technical expertise required for this ministry/activity?
5. Are we able to fund this ministry/activity in a sustainable manner?
6. Do we have or can we create the capacity for this ministry/activity?

Step 3. Identify and Evaluate Pathway Activities

Once you have your WHOM identified and your Pathway Conduit selected, you're ready to start identifying and evaluating ministries and activities that are appropriate for this WHOM. Begin by identifying existing ministries and activities that are of interest to and appealing to your WHOM. Then discuss some new ministries and activities that may provide more opportunities for engaging the nonchurched people in your community, especially the WHOM under consideration. Don't worry about classifying the activities yet. Instead, take time to brainstorm outreach ideas.

Capture the ministries and activities that you identify in some way. One way that works well is to write each one on a sticky note. Recording potential Pathway Activities on individual sticky notes is a handy way to sort, evaluate, and classify your ideas. Sticky notes can be easily rearranged on the Outreach Funnel and on Outreach Pathways. As you capture the ideas, clearly indicate the phase that the activity best fits. For example, mark an activity with "NR" if it belongs to the Nurture Relationships phase.

After you've captured all your ideas, evaluate them one at a time,5 using the seven questions for evaluating Pathway Activities. Use the Outreach Funnel to organize the activities that have the potential to be effective Pathway Activities based on your evaluation. Set aside any ministry or activity that doesn't evaluate well for this WHOM and Pathway Conduit so you can revisit them for other WHOMs and conduits.

QUESTIONS FOR EVALUATING PATHWAY ACTIVITIES		
Question	**Phase(s) of Outreach Process**	**Focus/Purpose**
1. What about this activity would WHOM find interesting or appealing?	All	Looking at outreach activities from the WHOM's perspective
2. How does this activity provide a way for our congregation to continue contact with WHOM?	Create Connections	Ensuring we have a means of continuing contact with WHOM
3. Why would WHOM be willing to participate in this activity?	All, especially Nurture Relationships	Considering obstacles that may keep an interested WHOM from participating
4. How does this activity help our members engage WHOM on an ongoing basis?	Nurture Relationships	Bringing members and our WHOM together repeatedly over time
5. How have we equipped our members for using this activity to nurture relationships with WHOM?	Nurture Relationships	Identifying ways to equip members for nurturing outreach relationships
6. To which entry points into the Word-and-Sacrament ministry of our congregation does this activity guide WHOM?	Make Disciples	Identifying entry points into Word-and-Sacrament ministry
7. Why would WHOM be interested in participating in the Word-and-Sacrament ministry of our congregation through this activity?	Make Disciples	Considering obstacles that may keep an interested WHOM from participating

Step 4. Arrange and Capture the Outreach Pathway

Place the Pathway Activities that you have evaluated and organized into the appropriate swim lanes on the Outreach Pathway. Remember to stay focused on the WHOM of the pathway by providing a logical sequence of activities that move your WHOM from a connection into relationship-building activities and then into the Word-and-Sacrament ministry of your congregation. As you arrange the activities, keep asking the question "What's next?" to guide you in creating the flow of the pathway.

After arranging the Pathway Activities on the Outreach Pathway, add lines from and to the activities to show the planned sequence of moving through the Outreach Process. Always maintain the flow of the pathway from left to right. Make sure that each swim lane has one and only one person assigned to it. Remember, you can assign a person to more than one swim lane if it helps to maintain the left-to-right flow of the pathway.

After the pathway is complete, look it over to identify and resolve any obstacles or gaps. The obstacles will be apparent where there is not a person assigned to a swim lane and where lines jump from Create Connections to Make Disciples. Gaps are present where a Pathway Activity does not have a line coming into it or a line leading to an activity that answers "What's next?" Of course, some Make Disciples activities may not have anything following them because they represent the end of the pathway.

Repeat these steps to create Outreach Pathways for the same WHOM with a different Pathway Conduit, a different WHOM with the same Pathway Conduit, a different WHOM with a different Pathway Conduit, and so on. Keep the pathways simple and straightforward by creating multiple pathways that are focused on a single WHOM for a specific Pathway Conduit.

POSTSCRIPT

After reading this book, some people may think, "That's a lot of work. Why can't we just put up a sign and welcome the people who show up?" I know that you could do that—after all, that's the way some congregations have done outreach for many years. But I hope you see that such an approach to outreach is not an effective way to engage the nonchurched people in your community. My guess is that you do. I hope that you've found a great deal of useful information in this book to help with your outreach efforts.

Outreach is a lot of work. The process, tools, and ideas in this book are meant to help you with that work. But that work is your work. You may find that some of the things in this book are not helpful in your context or that you have a different way of doing the same thing. That's fine. Use what you can, change what you need, and add your own ideas. Make the process, tools, and ideas presented here into things that work for you and your congregation.

My desired outcome for this book is not that you or everyone else does outreach the way that I've described it but that you would have a process, tools, and ideas to aid you in engaging the nonchurched people around you. It's my hope that this book will foster discussions, encourage action, and motivate people to get involved in more effective outreach to the glory of our Savior, Jesus, and the good of the people around you who are in great need of His love and grace.

May you be blessed and be a blessing as you start or continue planning and conducting intentional outreach to engage your lost and perishing neighbors with the Good News of Jesus.

DISCUSSION QUESTIONS

Chapter 1

1. In what ways does the example of the Oregon Stamp Society reflect how our congregation has been doing outreach?

2. How have the nonchurched people in our community responded to the signs and advertisements that tell them they are welcome at our congregation? Why have they responded in these ways?

3. What is your reaction to Martin Luther's statement that Christians should be called "priests"?

4. In what ways have you acted as a mediator between your neighbors and Christ?

Chapter 2

1. How is the distinction between witness as the work of the Church Scattered and outreach as the work of the Church Gathered helpful to you?

2. Based on the definition of outreach in chapter 2, what activities in our congregation have we been calling "outreach" that are not actually outreach?

3. Which part of the definition of outreach do you find most helpful? Which part do you find challenging?

4. Why is showing the love of Jesus through mercy work or human care ministries not in and of itself outreach? Which activities that we've been considering as outreach fall into this category?

Chapter 3

1. Which of the characteristics of effective outreach is the most helpful to you? How is it helpful?

2. Which of the characteristics of effective outreach is the most challenging to you? What makes it challenging?

3. In what ways are the members of our congregation like the people in the community around our church? In what ways are they different?

4. Have you ever been the target of a bait-and-switch tactic? If so, how did it affect your relationship with the person/organization that used it?

5. How does the reality that it is the Holy Spirit who makes disciples by working faith when and where He wills affect your understanding of your role in outreach?

Chapter 4

1. What makes understanding the perspective of nonchurched people difficult for you?

2. How do the nonchurched people in our neighborhood view our church?

3. How has our neighborhood changed over the past five years? Ten years?

4. If our congregation closed tomorrow, how would the nonchurched people in our community be affected?

5. What are we willing to change to "be all things to all people"? What aren't we willing to change?

Chapter 5

1. What are we currently doing to Build Awareness? What's working well? What needs improvement?

2. How do we capture the contact information of nonchurched people who attend our events? What do we do with it?

3. Who are the people in our congregation who are naturally good at starting and developing relationships?

4. What do we need to do to equip and encourage more of our members to be active in nurturing outreach relationships?

5. What are the current entry points into our Word-and-Sacrament ministry? What can we do to offer additional entry points?

6. What makes an entry point into Word-and-Sacrament ministry appropriate for nonchurched people? What is an example of an inappropriate entry point?

Chapter 6

1. How does visualizing the Outreach Process as a sideways funnel help you better understand how the Outreach Process works?

2. What would it look like if we were to draw our current outreach efforts as a sideways funnel?

3. What can we do to increase the number of people who progress from the Build Awareness to the Create Connections phases of the Outreach Process?

4. What can we do to reduce the number of people who drop out of the Outreach Process during the Nurture Relationships phase?

5. How does the Outreach Funnel emphasize the importance of being intentional in outreach? How intentional are our current outreach efforts?

Chapter 7

1. How is having a "map" for outreach helpful for the people involved in planning outreach? The people who are carrying out the planned outreach activities?

2. Why is it important to create unique pathways for each specific type of nonchurched person we are trying to engage through our outreach efforts?

3. Are our current outreach efforts best described as focused on a specific type of nonchurched person, one-size-fits-all, or something in between?

4. What obstacles are keeping nonchurched people from becoming disciples in our current outreach efforts?

5. What gaps are nonchurched people falling through after they make an initial connection with our congregation?

6. How might planning intentional outreach through Outreach Pathways help us reduce obstacles and gaps?

Chapter 8

1. On which specific types of nonchurched people have we focused our current outreach efforts?

2. What specific types of nonchurched people make up our community?

3. How should we differentiate between unchurched and dechurched people in our outreach efforts?

4. How can we do a better job of looking at the things that we are doing for outreach from the perspective of the nonchurched people in our community?

5. What outreach have we done that isn't local? How can we make use of those experiences to do local outreach?

Chapter 9

1. Which of our current ministries and activities are good candidates for serving as Pathway Conduits? How could they be good conduits?

2. Why is it important to consider a WHOM when selecting a Pathway Conduit?

3. How would we determine if there is room in our community for us to start a new ministry or activity to use as a Pathway Conduit?

4. When have we voted for a new ministry or activity that never got off the ground because there wasn't enough interest or support in the congregation?

5. What are some of the sources of technical expertise for new ministries and activities that we haven't made use of?

6. How are finances, facilities, or equipment needs affecting our ability to start or conduct ministries or activities that could be effective Pathway Conduits?

Chapter 10

1. Which of our existing ministries or activities would be good Pathway Activities for Creating Connections? Nurturing Relationships? Making Disciples?

2. What ideas for new ministries or activities have we discussed in the past that would be good Pathway Activities?

3. What helps you put yourself in the place a nonchurched person to better understand which activities of our congregation would be of interest and appealing?

4. Why do we need to evaluate Pathway Activities with a specific WHOM in mind?

5. What resources are you familiar with that would be helpful for equipping our members to Nurture Relationships?

6. What do we need to consider when we are creating entry points into our Word-and-Sacrament ministry that a WHOM would find of interest?

Chapter 11

1. When have you had to use a guide, map, or plan that looked like a "spaghetti chart"?

2. Why are some people tempted to do the planning for ministries or activities included on a pathway rather than identifying the outreach efforts that make up the pathway? How is that a temptation for you?

3. How is "who ensures what" different from "who does what"? Which are you more comfortable with?

4. What did you like about Grace Lutheran Church and School's Outreach Pathway? What didn't you like about it?

5. What did you like about Emmanuel Lutheran Church and School's Outreach Pathway? What didn't you like about it?

Chapter 12

1. Who are the nonchurched people in your community? Build a chart to create a comprehensive listing.

2. Pick a WHOM from your list of nonchurched people, using SNAIL. How does having a list help pick a WHOM? How is using SNAIL helpful?

3. Identify an existing ministry or activity that can be used as a Pathway Conduit. What is the benefit of using the "Questions for Assessing a Pathway Conduit" to evaluate your selection?

4. Identify existing ministries and activities that can be used as Pathway Activities; determine which phases of the Outreach

Process each one belongs to. Which phases of the Outreach Process have an adequate number of activities to create a pathway? For which phases of the Outreach Process do we need to create new ministries and activities?

5. Arrange and capture a pathway. Where are the obstacles or gaps in our pathway? How do we resolve them?

GLOSSARY

Activity Things that the congregation does as one-time events, recurring events, projects, or ongoing endeavors.

Build Awareness The first phase of the Outreach Process, in which the congregation uses available marketing and advertising tools to inform the community of its presence, ministries, and activities.

Church Gathered The things congregational members do together, such as worship.

Church Scattered The work congregational members do when separated from one another, such as in homes, neighborhoods, or workplaces.

Create Connections The second phase of the Outreach Process, in which the congregation engages the nonchurched people in its community in ways that enable the congregation to continue contact with them.

dechurched A nonchurched person who was once connected to a Christian church but, for one reason or another, is no longer connected to a Christian church.

Make Disciples The fourth phase of the Outreach Process, in which the congregation provides entry points into its Word-and-Sacrament ministry that are interesting, appealing, and appropriate for the nonchurched people being invited.

Means of Grace The instruments that God uses to give spiritual blessings; namely, His Word, Holy Baptism, and the Lord's Supper.

ministry In a narrow sense, activities in the congregation that are directly related to the proclamation and teaching of God's Word and the administration of His Sacraments. In a wide sense, the various functions of a congregation, including events and activities that are not directly related to Word and Sacrament.

nonchurched People who are not currently connected to a Christian church. The nonchurched include those who have no faith, those who have left the faith, and those who confess a non-Christian religion.

Nurture Relationships The third phase of the Outreach Process, in which the congregation works through ministries and activities to build Outreach Relationships with nonchurched people.

outreach	Our congregation's efforts to make disciples by engaging the nonchurched people in our community through our ministries and activities in order to share the Gospel of Jesus Christ with them.
Outreach Funnel	A diagram of the Outreach Process presented as a sideways funnel divided into four sections, each of which represents a phase of the Outreach Process.
Outreach Pathway	A plan for helping nonchurched people through the Outreach Process that captures a series of activities arranged in a logical sequence from Create Connections to Nurture Relationships to Make Disciples.
Outreach Process	A defined series of steps used to organize outreach efforts into specific phases, each with its own focus and purpose. The four phases of the Outreach Process discussed in this book are Build Awareness, Create Connections, Nurture Relationships, and Make Disciples.
outreach relationship	A professional relationship between a nonchurched person and a member or members of our congregation.
Pathway Activity	A ministry or activity of the congregation that is included in an Outreach Pathway.
Pathway Conduit	A ministry or activity of the congregation that provides entry points into an Outreach Pathway, especially one that provides a means to Create Connections with nonchurched people.
SNAIL	An acronym describing the attributes of a WHOM. The letters stand for **S**pecific, **N**onchurched, **A**ccessible, **I**nterested, and **L**ocal.
unchurched	A nonchurched person who has never been connected to a Christian church, including people who are active in non-Christian religions.
WHOM	An acronym that describes a specific type of nonchurched person on whom we are focusing our outreach efforts. The letters stand for **W**ho **H**as **O**ur **M**ission focus.
witness	The work we do individually as disciples of Jesus to speak of Him with nonchurched people in the context of our everyday lives.
Word-and-Sacrament ministry	The activities of the congregation through which we hear and study God's Word and receive His Sacraments.